Good Fishing in the Adirondacks

From Lake Champlain to the Streams of Tug Hill

Third Edition

Dennis Aprill

THE COUNTRYMAN PRESS

WOODSTOCK, VERMONT

With time, access points may change, and road numbers, signs, and landmarks referred to in this book may be altered. If you find that such changes have occurred near the streams described in this book, please let the author and publisher know, so that corrections may be made in future editions. Other comments and suggestions are also welcome. Address all correspondence to:

Fishing Editor
The Countryman Press
P.O. Box 748
Woodstock, VT 05091

Library of Congress Cataloging-in-Publication Data are available

Good Fishing in the Adirondacks
ISBN 978-0-88150-891-8

Interior photographs by the author unless otherwise specified
Maps by Larry Boutis, Jim Capossela, and Jacques Chazaud, © The Countryman Press
Book design by Faith Hague
Composition by Eugenie S. Delaney

Published by The Countryman Press, P.O. Box 748, Woodstock, VT 05091
Distributed by W. W. Norton & Company, Inc., 500 Fifth Avenue, New York, NY 10110
Printed in the United States of America

10 9 8 7 6 5 4 3 2 1

Good Fishing
in the
Adirondacks

The Good Fishing in New York Series

Contents

List of Maps

Map Legend

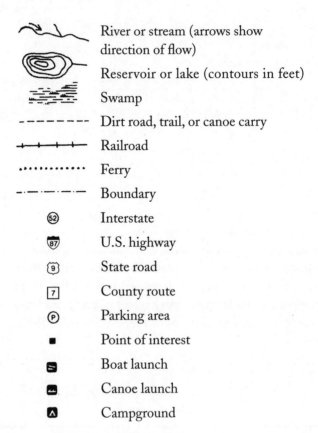

River or stream (arrows show direction of flow)

Reservoir or lake (contours in feet)

Swamp

Dirt road, trail, or canoe carry

Railroad

Ferry

Boundary

Interstate

U.S. highway

State road

County route

Parking area

Point of interest

Boat launch

Canoe launch

Campground

Preface to the Third Edition

Good Fishing in the Adirondacks first came out in 1990, and there have been many changes since then. These changes are reflected in this new, overhauled, and updated edition. Among the additions are new information on the threats from invasive species and measures the Department of Environmental Conservation has taken to halt this invasion. Within the chapters about fishing in Lake Champlain, Lake George, the Ausable and Saranac rivers, the St. Lawrence, and many Adirondack waters in between, we have included the latest information about fish ladders, lamprey control programs, fish stocking, fishing techniques and regulations, as well as new suggestions for fishing in the backcountry, finding landlocked salmon, and other highlights of the region.

When I was first asked to write an Adirondack fishing guide 20 years ago, a guide that would include virtually all of New York north of the Thruway—or to put it in perspective, an area larger than Vermont, Rhode Island, and Connecticut combined—I realized no one person could claim honestly to be an expert on every aspect of such a vast area; so I called upon fishing guides, outdoor writers, members of Trout Unlimited, and other local experts to share their fishing knowledge as contributors. My thanks go to them. Rest assured, you are getting the best possible advice.

I hope you enjoy the new edition.

DENNIS APRILL

Dennis Aprill with a couple of large brook trout.

About the Editor

Dennis Aprill is a licensed New York State guide (#1474) and member of the New York State Outdoor Writers Association. He has fished extensively in northern New York and Canada. He has been the outdoors columnist for the Plattsburgh *Press-Republican* since 1990, and a frequent contributor to *Adirondack Life* magazine. Books he has authored are the *Paths Less Traveled* and *Short Treks in the Adirondacks and Beyond* Adirondack hiking guides, and *Mammals of the Adirondacks* (coauthor). When not fishing and writing, Dennis teaches English classes at the State University of New York, Plattsburgh. In 2009, he was inducted into the New York State Outdoorsmen Hall of Fame and is the 2003 Trout Unlimited New York Communicator of the Year. He lives with his wife in a remote section of the eastern Adirondacks.

Introduction

Imagine for a moment that you are suspended 30,000 feet directly above Mount Marcy, New York State's highest mountain. The high peaks appear as a somewhat off-center hub of a gigantic wheel, with rivers radiating from them like spokes toward every point on the compass. Flowing north are the Raquette and St. Regis; to the east the Saranac, Ausable, and Boquet; to the south the Schroon and the Hudson; and to the west the Moose and the Beaver. From this preferred vantage point, not only would you start to get an idea of the immensity and wildness of the region, but a peculiar geological truth might sneak into your consciousness: The Adirondacks are a large dome eroded away (though certainly not uniformly) in every direction by flowing water.

If the day were especially clear, you might even be treated to the sight of two gigantic lakes to the east and south; to a spiderweb of streams laced across an elevated land mass to the southwest; to a huge river to the northwest. Lake George, Lake Champlain, Tug Hill, the St. Lawrence River—all these tempting possibilities might come into view. And then another reality would hit home: There is an awful lot of water just outside the Adirondacks—in all directions, as a matter of fact.

This book, then, is about fishing in northern New York, roughly that area north of the New York Thruway. It focuses not only on the wild and beautiful central Adirondacks, but also on the vast water systems on the fringes. Through the voices of local writers, all of whom live in northern New York and many of whom were born here, this book takes you to remote brook trout ponds and intimate streams, leads you to larger blue-ribbon fly-fishing rivers, and guides you to crystalline lakes with lake trout, salmon, bass, muskie, pike, and much more.

With a culture and a history both unique and varied, this great wilderness of the east has been consecrated by artists in every possible medium: photography, painting, poetry, mountain crafts, and, of course, writing. It is still a beautiful, lightly settled region—only 120,000 people live full-time within the Adirondack Blue Line—and it's so inspiring that a modern-day angler might yet share the sentiments of W. H. H. "Adirondack" Murray, who described in *Adventures in the Wilderness* the first morning of an

Adirondack fishing adventure more than a century ago: "How cool the water; how fresh the air; how clear the sky; how fragrant the breath of balsam and pine; O luxury of luxuries, to have a lake of crystal water for your wash bowl, the morning zephyr for a towel, the whitest sand for soap and the odor of aromatic trees for perfumes! What belle or millionaire can boast of such surroundings?"

We hope this book will share with you some of the vast potential and astonishing diversity of fishing in the Adirondack region and will lead you to many enjoyable adventures. If you have suggestions, comments, or corrections for future editions of the guide, please write to Dennis Aprill, c/o The Countryman Press, P.O. Box 748, Woodstock, VT 05091.

A Note on the Maps

Because of the limiting size of a book page and the scale of the area being drawn, only very select points of interest are depicted on the maps in this book. We have not been able to show all secondary roads or access trails. Please use an atlas for navigation in getting to the lakes and rivers, and use these maps to better understand the text and provide a starting point for trip planning.

Some Facts about Acid Rain

One of the big environmental problems of our age, along with and associated with climate change, is acid rain, also called acid deposition. The Adirondacks is one of the areas of North America that has been hardest hit by this insidious menace, and the publicity has led many anglers to believe that most Adirondack waters are "dead." This is far from the case, since good fishing still abounds in stream and pond, lake and river. Yet it is true that about two hundred high-elevation ponds here have been wiped out by acid rain and that about three hundred more are threatened. In addition, certain headwater tributary streams have been affected to the point that fish life has been greatly diminished or even eradicated.

Acid rain stems from the chemical reaction of sulfur and nitrogen oxides with water in the atmosphere. These chemicals are primarily released into the atmosphere via the smokestacks of factories and the tailpipes of motorized vehicles. Basic high school chemistry demonstrates that when you combine the oxides of these chemicals with H_2O, you get H_2SO_4 and HNO_3, or sulphuric acid and nitric acid. It literally rains (and snows) acid. Not only has this hurt aquatic life, but it is now starting to slowly kill some of our higher-elevation forests. It is safe to assume that as acid rain worsens—and the woeful "wait and see" attitude of the federal government has assured that it will—its direct impact on human health will be exacerbated.

The relative acidity or alkalinity of any solution depends on its concentration of hydrogen ions. It is expressed as a number on a logarithmic scale ranging from 0 to 14.0. A pH of 7.0 is neutral. A change of one pH unit, for example from 6.0 to 5.0, indicates a tenfold increase in hydrogen ion concentration. Normal rainwater is 5.6, and the pH of acid rain is lower. How much lower determines the magnitude of the threat. In the mid-1970s, the mean pH of 214 high-elevation Adirondack ponds was about 4.75. Some species can tolerate (at least in the short term) this degree of acidity, but most cannot. Anything below 5.0 is generally bad news.

And that leads us to the classifications used in dealing with acid rain. Waters having a pH of 6.0 or higher are considered "satisfactory." Those between 5.0 and 6.0 are considered "endangered." Those below 5.0 are termed "critical."

In a synoptic chemistry survey that took place between 1975 and 1982, 1,047 Adirondack lakes and ponds were sampled. This is about 38 percent of the 2,759 ponded waters located within the region (transitory beaver and bog ponds would push that 2,759 figure higher). All the sampled waters fell within a modified 1,000-foot elevation perimeter, which roughly coincides with the Adirondack Park boundary. Approximately 92 percent of the estimated 246,271 acres of ponded water within the zone were sampled. The results were as follows:

Waters	(%)	Classification	Acres	(%)
199	(19.0)	Critical (below 5.0 pH)	8,796	(3.9)
264	(25.2)	Endangered (5.0–6.0 pH)	23,346	(10.3)
584	(55.8)	Satisfactory (above 6.0 pH)	193,710	(85.8)

Surveys done by the Adirondack Lake Survey Corporation covered 1,469 ponds or lakes. Of these, 1,123 contained fish, and 346 were without fish. In looking at these two surveys, though, it should be remembered that some of the now-fishless ponds undoubtedly never did contain fish.

In spite of that qualifier, there is no denying that acid rain has either wiped out or reduced the fishing opportunity on about 25 percent of fishable Adirondack ponds. The surveys have shown that ponds smaller than 20 acres and at elevations greater than 2,000 feet are at greatest risk. Though less studied at this point, certain smaller streams at higher elevations have also been seriously affected. Taking a region-wide look, we see that waters in the southwestern Adirondacks have been hardest hit. This is partially because of higher precipitation levels in this part of the Adirondacks. As an example, many ponds and lakes just north of Stillwater Reservoir, including ones in the scenic Five Ponds Area, have been strongly affected.

Backpacking in for native brook trout is an old Adirondack tradition and is well covered in this book. Yet it is clear from the preceding discussion that an angler heading out into the mountains by foot or by canoe should find out which ponds to avoid. Here, the New York State Department of Environmental Conservation (DEC) can help.

Regional DEC offices in Ray Brook, Warrensburg, and Watertown (see Resources for contact information) can provide specific information on most waters within their jurisdiction for which current survey data exists.

There have been other changes since the first edition of this book two decades ago. One is the proliferation of invasive species like alewives in Lake Champlain, and *Didymosphenia geminata,* or didymo, a mucky, fast-spreading algae that coats the bottom of streams, destroying fish habitat. It is also called rock snot and is, unfortunately, now found in some Adirondack streams. The use of nonnative or diseased baitfish has forced the DEC to require that anglers only use live baitfish in the area where it is collected or that anglers buy certified baitfish from a state-approved dealer. Though it seems a bit harsh, this restriction is necessary to protect the fishery.

A Note of Caution

The New York State Department of Health warns that some fish in New York waters contain certain potentially harmful contaminants. This is not true of all waters and fish in the Adirondacks, however. You are advised to consult the New York State DEC for further details before eating any fish you may catch. Many of the current advisories will be on the inside of the front cover of the DEC annual publication *New York State Fishing Regulations Guide,* or go to the DEC Web site at www.dec.ny.gov.

Catch-and-Release

No one will argue that a fish fry makes for a great shore lunch or dinner, and catching a trophy-sized fish and having it mounted is, for some, a remembrance of a great fishing trip; however, there is no need to keep more fish than you will eat. Catch-and-release should be a regular practice thereafter. To ease a release, use single barbless hooks, don't overplay the fish, and get it back into the water as quickly as possible. There is still usually time to take a photo.

Colin Aprill, at age seven, with a lake trout.

CHAPTER ONE

Lake Champlain: Warm-Water Species

Ricky Doyle

L ake Champlain is one of the largest freshwater lakes in the United States. It is nestled between the beautiful Adirondack Mountains of New York and the Green Mountains of Vermont. Rich in both history and beauty, Champlain has been referred to by some of the world's greatest anglers as "a little piece of heaven." Yet with its immense size and opportunities, one would hardly consider it "little." Although there is much data available, it is better to give approximate figures, as it seems that most of them vary from source to source. The lake area of 435 square miles boasts 587 miles of shoreline, with an average depth of 64 feet. The greatest lake depth (approximately 400 feet) is found between Charlotte, Vermont, and Essex, New York—not, as one would expect, at its widest point (12 miles), between Burlington, Vermont, and Port Kent, New York.

The immense size makes it a haven for a variety of recreational activities, from swimming, diving, sailing, fishing, Jet Skiing, and wind surfing in the open-water months to numerous ice sports during the winter. Activity on the lake has changed, with new interest in numerous sporting activities surfacing in recent years. With these new interests, there is ample opportunity for

Karalyn Aprill with Lake Champlain bass.
Champlain is one of the nation's best bass fisheries.

everyone to enjoy what Lake Champlain has to offer year-round.

Yet with all that the lake has to offer, there are concerns for anglers. The big lake has an imaginary line that goes down the middle, dividing it between two states. There is also a small portion of it that lies in Canada. Due to this, it is best to have maps and charts before you head out. Although there is now a reciprocal fishing license agreement between Vermont and New York, there are strict regulations on the use of it. All anglers should familiarize themselves with these regulations before venturing out on the open waters.

Fishing on Lake Champlain

In this chapter we will be dealing with the warm-water species of Lake Champlain (the cold-water species are discussed in chapter 2). I'll be discussing the western shore of Champlain from Whitehall, New York, all the way to the Canadian border.

Before we start, I would like to pass along a bit of advice if you plan to fish the lake from a boat: be sure to have properly working safety equipment. The many years I have spent on the lake have taught me that water that looks like a sheet of glass one minute can become a small white-capped sea the next.

Fishing opportunities abound on Lake Champlain. You have a wide variety of fish no other fishery in the northeast can match. We will deal mainly with the most popular species: large- and smallmouth bass, northern pike, walleye, pickerel, muskellunge, and some of the popular panfish.

We will begin our fishing in the southern part of Lake Champlain near Whitehall and work our way north to Rouses Point.

In South Bay, fish top water plastic frogs around water chestnut, and follow up a missed bite with a Texas rig black 4-inch tube by flipping it to the exact spot where the bass rolled on the top water. This same technique works in all the small bays and cuts from South Bay all the way to the fort in Ticonderoga. These bays include Red Rock, Peters, Pickerel, Mill, Benson, Stevens, Rocky, Catfish, and Galax Marsh. All of these areas also have some fair-sized pike around them. A white spinnerbait used around the opening in the chestnut will serve you well.

From the Fort in Ticonderoga to Port Henry

In this area, the lake has larger bays with less chestnut and more milfoil that the bass and pike prefer. These bays include Stoney Cove, Laphams Bay, Leonards Bay, Monitor Bay, Girard's, and Bulwagga. The bass love the milfoil. In these bays, in 4 to 8 feet of water, flipping jigs and soft plastics in the milfoil will produce some great catches. A 1-ounce black and blue jig with plastic trailer will work just great; also, top water baits such as buzz baits in white or yellow, plastic frogs and flukes, and white spinnerbaits. Crankbaits that dive 3 to 7 feet work well on the outside edges of the same weed beds. There are two small rivers and two small creeks that dump into the lake in the area that good bass and pike and can be caught in: Poultney River, LaChute River, East Creek, and Putman Creek. Plastic worms such as a senko unweighted and top water frogs work well in all four areas. Both fished around the thick cover. There are also many small points in this area of the lake that hold bass and pike, including Gourlie, Larabes, Kerby, Watch, Five Mile, Yellow House, and Chimney Points. Fishing off the end of these points

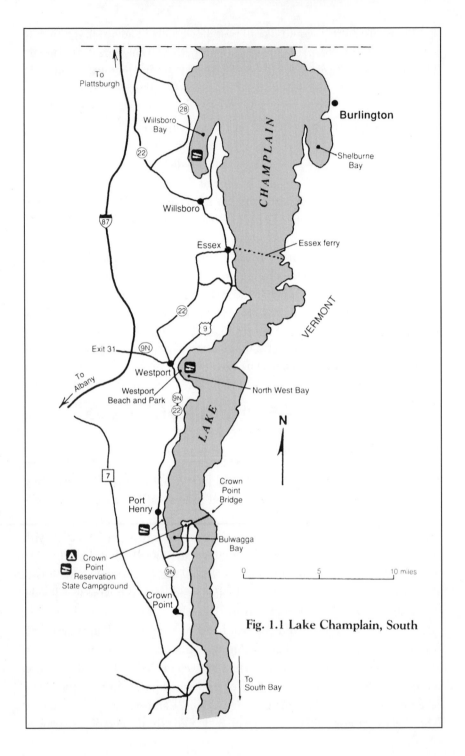

Fig. 1.1 Lake Champlain, South

in 4 to 10 feet of water with white and chartreuse medium diving crankbaits, jerkbaits, and spinnerbaits will work great for bass and pike. On windy days these points can be great for fishing. All of the areas talked about in this section of the lake are on both the New York and Vermont side because the lake is so narrow there. For the remainder of the lake, we will be writing about only the New York side, as the lake gets much wider there.

Westport to Plattsburgh

This part of the lake is not only the widest, but also the deepest. The bass and pike fishing in this area is not as good as the other sections of the lake; however, bass and pike can be caught in bays such as North West, Hunter, Rock Harbor, Whallon, and Willsboro. They can also be caught around the Ausable Point area, the Ausable River, Valcour Island, and Cumberland Bay. Smallmouth bass hold on the rocky drop-offs in these areas. Top water baits, drop shotting, larger chartreuse and white spinnerbaits, and Carolina rig plastic such as worm leeches would be the best way to land some of the holding fish. Pike can be caught on spinner-, jerk-, and crankbaits, all in perch colors. This area of the lake has great yellow perch fishing year-round. Use small jigs with trailers and live minnows. Willsboro Bay and Cumberland Bay are great choices for fishing perch, especially in the winter months.

Plattsburgh to Rouses Point

Treadwell, Middle, Deep, Monty, Trombley, Kings, Catfish—all have one thing in common: They are some of the best bays for fishing in the northern end of the lake. We also can't forget the Great Chazy River and the old railroad bridge in Rouses Point. This section of the lake has great bass, pike, and panfish fishing and some good muskellunge fishing. Since 2001, bass pros have discovered what a fantastic bass fishery Lake Champlain is, and numerous tournaments are held out of Plattsburgh each summer. The big lake has become a key destination for FLW, B.A.S.S., as well as smaller local tournaments.

Treadwell Bay

Just north of Cumberland Bay is a large bay called Treadwell, inside of which are two smaller bays—Middle and Deep. The smallmouth bass fishing in these bays is superb. Around the rocky points and the reefs in the middle of

Treadwell are large schools of smallies. Best baits in this area include top water baits imitating small perch, spinnerbaits, and jigs with crawfish-color trailers. Best depth range is from 5 feet to 20 feet of water. You will also pick up some good pike around these bays on the same lures. Perch fishing is also great in these three bays year-round. The best way to catch these perch would be on small jigs and live minnows fished around 15 to 25 feet of water.

Monty Bay

We'll now move into Monty Bay. This bay has great bass, pike, and panfish. Both small- and largemouth bass can be caught in this bay on the rocky points, in the weeds, and in the small marshy area in the south side of the bay. The largemouth bass can be caught on top water lures such as frogs, swimbaits, or jigs and trailers in crawfish colors. Also, 6-inch plastic worms such as Senkos and Zoom worms in black and green pumpkin colors work well fished around weed beds and lily pads in 2 to 3 feet of water. The small-mouth can be caught on all the rocky points around the bay on top water in perch-color spinnerbaits and in chartreuse and green pumpkin tube jigs. They can also be caught in the weed beds in 15 to 20 feet of water. Around the weeds, big spinnerbaits and jerkbaits in perch pattern seem to work well. Using large live minnows will produce some great catches of pike. Monty Bay has a large concentration of perch and sunfish, which can be caught on live minnows and worms from 2 to 20 feet of water.

Trombley Bay

Trombley Bay is great for smallmouth and perch fishing, but you will pick up an occasional largemouth bass and pike while fishing here. Rocks around weeds are the key to this bay; where the rocks and the weeds meet is where the smallmouth and perch tend to stay. Small jigs in crawfish color, 6-inch worms in green pumpkin color, and live minnows will all catch the bass and perch.

Kings Bay

Reaching Kings Bay, which is situated at the mouth of the Chazy River, we find some of the greatest bass, pike, muskie, and panfish anywhere on the lake. Let's start with the muskie. In late spring to early summer, the muskie come into the river to spawn. They are a challenge but can be caught on large spinnerbaits, jerkbaits, and top water baits fished fast and erratic to look like a large wounded minnow along the weed edges and in the deep holes of the river.

Pike fishing in this area is not limited to any specific time of year. Some nice pike can be caught year-round in Kings Bay and in the spring in the mouth of the Chazy River. Live bait like shiner minnows work best, but the pike can be caught on lures such as large spoons like a Dardevle, spinnerbaits, jerkbaits, and large jigs all fished around the weed edges in 2 to 10 feet of water.

The bass fishing in this area is some of the best in the lake during the entire bass season. In the spring the bass start moving into the shallow sections of the bay and the river, and all spring long and during the early summer you can catch them around weeds, rocks, and wood. Use plastic worms, jigs and trailers, and top water baits. As summer arrives, the bass move deeper and can be caught offshore in around 8½ to 10 feet of water where rocks and weeds come together.

Panfish here consists of yellow perch, sunfish, bluegill, and crappie, all of which can be caught year-round in 2 to 10 feet of water using live minnows or worms and small jigs around the outside of the weed beds.

Catfish Bay

As we move into Catfish Bay, one must not underestimate its size. Although considered small in comparison to other bays, it holds large schools of perch, sunfish, bluegill, and crappie. Best fishing for these panfish is early spring through midsummer, in from 2 to 8 feet of water with live minnows and worms or small jigs. The bay also holds pike and bass, mostly from early spring to early summer. Both can be caught around weeds and rocks on plastic worms and live minnows.

Rouses Point

Fishing in the Rouses Point area focuses around the old railroad bridge and the many submerged cribs around the point waterfront. The cribs and the waterfront are comprised mainly of rock and wood, with weeds growing all around them. Bass and pike are always feeding along the edges, so try top water early and plastic worms as it gets later in the day. Probably the most famous section of the lake's northern end is the old wooden railroad bridge in the village of Rouses Point. The old wooden pilings go across the narrow part of the lake in that area, and both small- and largemouth bass live and feed in the sunken wood there year-round, with the occasional large pike. The best bass fishing starts in midsummer and lasts until mid-October. Texas rigged plastic worms, large jigs and trailers, and Texas rigged tubes work best around the wood. Be prepared to lose lots of tackle, but it will be worth it for these catches.

About the Author

Ricky Doyle has spent many years on Lake Champlain fishing in all seasons. An avid ice fisherman as well as a former tournament bass pro angler, he has competed on both state and national levels, fishing both the B.A.S.S. and FLW Stren circuits. He started with the New York State Bass Federation and made the New York State team on numerous occasions, and he is a past NYS Federation Angler of the Year. Ricky makes his home in Keeseville, New York, and still enjoys fishing as one of his favorite pastimes.

CHAPTER TWO

Lake Champlain: Cold-Water Species

Peter Casamento

The preceding chapter offers much information on the impressive dimensions of Lake Champlain and its primary warm-water species. Well, this extraordinary body of water may be the ultimate two-story fishery. Let's now look at the stellar fishing that can be had here for cold-water species.

Lake Champlain probably has as many or more different types of catchable freshwater fish as any lake in the Northeast. Landlocked salmon, lake trout, brown trout, rainbow trout, smelt, and whitefish are the main cold-water species, and these primarily inhabit the middle two-thirds of the lake. Lake trout and salmon are the most abundant of these game fish. Hundreds of thousands of lakers and landlocks are stocked each year by New York and Vermont. In addition, fall salmon runs on some rivers and have established some natural reproduction.

Lakers average 3 to 8 pounds, and a lot of lunkers weighing more than 10 pounds are caught. The salmon average 2 to 4 pounds, but mixed in are quite a few 6- to 8-pounders and an occasional trophy more than 10 pounds.

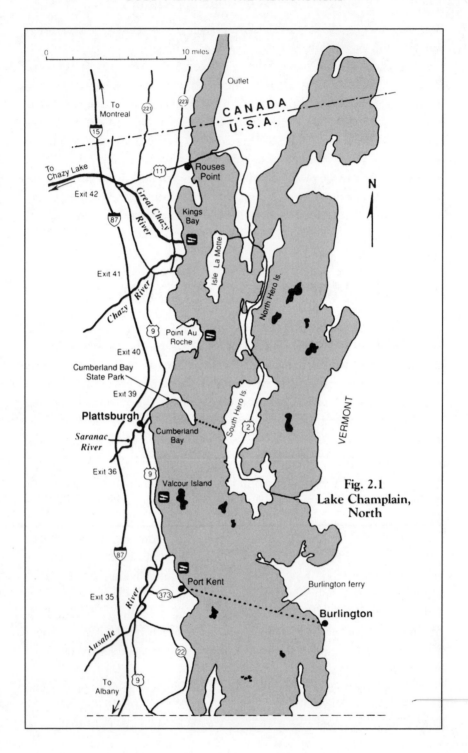

0   10 miles

Outlet

To Montreal

221

223

CANADA
U.S.A.

15

N

To Chazy Lake

11

Rouses Point

Exit 42

87

Great Chazy River

Kings Bay

Isle La Motte

North Hero Is

Exit 41

Chazy River

9

Point Au Roche

Exit 40

Cumberland Bay State Park

Exit 39

South Hero Is

VERMONT

Plattsburgh

Saranac River

Cumberland Bay

2

Exit 36

9

Valcour Island

Fig. 2.1
Lake Champlain,
North

87

Port Kent

Burlington ferry

Exit 35

373

Ausable River

Burlington

22

To Albany

9

30

Both rainbows (steelhead) and browns average 2 to 4 pounds, with an occasional 6- to 8-pound fish.

The states of New York and Vermont began the Sea Lamprey Control Project on Lake Champlain in the 1980s, with chemical lampricides applied in all the major rivers running into Lake Champlain. The effect of those treatments in the '80s and '90s was so successful that Lake Champlain was considered by many to be the premier lake for landlocked salmon and lake trout in the country. But then, when the state of Vermont suddenly stopped the treatments, it wasn't long before the bottom fell out. Even though there was a 10-year environmental impact study done on the effects of using lampricide before it was implemented on Champlain, certain environmental groups put a stop to the treatments on the Vermont side of Champlain. The treatments were stopped for quite a few years, enough to almost completely undo the earlier successes. Due to petitions and pressure from many sportsmens' groups and others, the treatments are once again being applied, and the trout and salmon populations are coming back fast.

The most abundant cold-water species is smelt. Though not considered a game fish, it is one of the most popular food fish among the natives and is the main diet of cold-water game fish. There are millions of smelt in Lake Champlain, and without them there would not be much of a cold-water fishery. Smelt average 4 to 8 inches but occasionally grow to longer than 12 inches.

Whitefish inhabit the deep-water areas of the lake. Although they are not stocked, there are a lot of these fish in Lake Champlain. Until recently, whitefish were seldom caught, and most anglers did not even know they were there. Fishing techniques used in other lakes across the country are now being used in Lake Champlain, and the whitefish is becoming a popular game fish, as well as a popular food fish. Whitefish average 2 to 4 pounds and can reach a weight of 20 pounds.

Alewives (a freshwater herring) are now abundant in Lake Champlain. They are a recent invasive species, probably brought in as bait. They are not a game fish or a food fish for humans, but they will have a profound effect on Lake Champlain fishing in years to come. No one knows what the outcome will be, but we do know that in many other lakes alewives have invaded, they have completely replaced the natural forage fish—and they will probably replace the smelt in Lake Champlain someday. On the other hand, other lakes, like the Great Lakes, have benefited from this. Salmon and trout of the Great Lakes grow to tremendous size because of the alewife, and maybe the trout and salmon of Lake Champlain will do the same, but only time will tell.

Spring

Ice-out on Lake Champlain is usually in late March or early April, and, like clockwork, the day the ice goes out, the salmon are in! This is the best time of the year for catching landlocked salmon in good numbers. These fish, along with browns and rainbows, concentrate in the mouths of the rivers, in or around the bays, and points near the mouths of the rivers. This time of year the rivers are high from melting snows, washing lots of food down to the lake. The river temperatures are also quite a bit warmer than the lake temperature; this warmer water really attracts the fish. At this time of year, while the waters are high and murky, anglers who troll or cast small bright spoons will be the most successful. For the live-bait angler, worms and night crawlers land the most fish.

About late April or early May, when the rains and melting snows have abated, the rivers and streams become crystal clear. This is the time for the lightest line and the smallest lures. Fly-casting streamers or trolling streamers with 2- to 4-pound test line will catch the most fish. For the bait fisherman, live or dead smelt is best. The best river- and stream-mouth areas for salmon and trout at this time of year are the Saranac, Ausable, Boquet, and Lachute rivers, and Putts Creek.

From ice-out until mid-May, lake trout and whitefish seem to be spread out in deep water. Anglers using downriggers or lead core line are the most successful. Whitefish are caught on very small spoons and spinners, while the lake trout tend to hit on much larger spoons and Rapala-type lures.

From mid-May until late June, the landlocks, rainbows, browns, and whitefish are found near the surface over deep-water areas. The areas from Point Au Roche to Port Henry on the New York side are the most productive parts of the lake for these species. Trolling spoons either by flatlining or by the use of planer boards is most productive. Lake trout seem to be at all depths at this time of year, and a lot of trout are caught right close to shore in a couple of feet of water near rocky points. Many anglers cast from shore or anchor their boats and cast to shore using ¼- to ¾-ounce jigs and spoons, while others use dead smelt fished just off the bottom. The most popular points for this shallow-water fishing are the Port Douglas to Port Kent area and the Willsboro Point to Westport area in New York. Anglers also enjoy success off the many islands and reefs in the lake at this time of year, especially Valcour Island, Schuyler Island, the Four Brothers Islands, Pumpkin Reef, Schuyler Reef, and Juniper and Diamond islands.

Setting downriggers for lake trout.

Summer

About late June, as the surface temperature of the lake rises, the salmon, trout, whitefish, and smelt go deep. Downrigger trolling, trolling with lead core line, deep-water jigging, or fishing near the bottom with live or dead smelt are the only ways to catch these fish during the summer. Though fish can be graphed more than 200 feet down, most fish are caught 40 to 120 feet down. Many different sizes and types of flutter spoons, spinners, and minnow imitating lures are used for deep-water trolling during the summer. The heavier spoons and bucktail jigs are used for jigging up lakers in deep water. During the hot summer months, finding the smelt grounds is the key to catching all the salmonids. Some of the major smelt areas are the deep-water areas off the mouths of the Ausable and Boquet rivers, Willsboro Bay/Pumpkin Reef area, Schuyler Reef/Four Brothers Island area, and the Whallon Bay to Westport area.

Next to winter ice fishing, this is the best time of year to catch smelt. Because most of the smelt are concentrated at different depths, jigging with small cut pieces of smelt is the most productive way to fill your bucket.

Fall

Fall is trophy time! Whether you dote on the cool-water species or the cold water, fall is the time for catching the biggest of what you're after.

About mid-September, when the air temperature drops below 70 degrees and the fall rains begin, the rivers and streams bring colder water down to Lake Champlain. The salmon, browns, and steelhead sense this and again swim upriver. At this time of year, these fish are not going up to feed, but to spawn. Even though the rivers and streams are high, Lake Champlain is around its lowest level of the year. This means that the lake does not back up the mouths of the rivers as it does in the spring, so there is not enough water in the rivers for boat fishing. All of the fishing is done from the banks or by

The result!

wading, using streamers, flies, worms, or minnows. Most salmon that go up-river in the fall are 4 pounds or larger.

Because these fish are on a spawning run, they are not feeding. Repeat-edly casting or drifting a fly or bait by them is the only way to get them to strike—out of instinct or aggravation. All in all, the success ratio at this time of year is lower than in the spring, even though the average size of the salmon caught is a lot bigger. Spawning continues through October and into early November. Afterward, most spent fish make their way back to the lake, where they once again start to feed. The Boquet, Saranac, and Ausable rivers are the very best fall bets for landlocks.

About mid-October, the surface temperature of Lake Champlain drops below 60 degrees, and once again there is great surface action for lake trout, whitefish, and the smaller browns, rainbows, and landlocks. In early No-vember, the bigger trout and salmon, which have completed their spawning runs, once again are feeding and are more easily caught. Early November through December is the time to catch the biggest lakers. Mature lake trout, which are 6 pounds or more, move into the shallow water to spawn at this time. Most spawning takes place in less than 10 feet of water. Unlike the other trout and salmon, unless they are actually in the act of spawning, lakers will take lures and bait readily. As in the spring, casting ¼- to ¾-ounce spoons will get the big lakers in the shallow water. Trolling flutter spoons, flies, and minnow-type lures will take the most salmon, rainbows, browns, and the smaller lake trout. Fall is probably the best time to get a lot of white-fish, and the right ticket is small spoons, flies, and spinners. Once again, as in the spring, most of these fish are caught in shallow water or near the surface over deep water. This action extends right to ice-over, which could be any-where from late December to mid-January.

Winter

Most parts of Champlain are frozen over by late January. Ice fishing for smelt, lakers, and salmon first starts around the Ticonderoga to Port Henry area. This area is just south of the deep-water smelt grounds, where the bottom comes up to about 40 feet. Here the lake is much shallower and freezes over a lot sooner. As soon as the ice is safe enough, the local anglers are out setting up their shanties, which are mainly used for smelt fishing. The anglers jig through holes in the floor of the shanties using hand lines. At the end of the line are one or two single hooks tipped with pieces of cut smelt;

above them is a 1-ounce or more pencil weight. This is the top method for catching smelt on Champlain.

With this method, some lake trout and salmon are taken incidentally; however, few local ice fishermen try for them. Lake Champlain is virtually untapped for this type of fishing. Tip-up fishing is probably the best way of getting lake trout and salmon in winter, and with state regulations allowing 15 tip-ups per person, an angler can cover a lot of territory. The best bait to use on the tip-ups is live or dead smelt fished from just under the ice to about 20 feet down. Jigging with special jigging Rapalas or with other types of ice jigs is the other way to take these fish.

Lures, Bait, and Tackle

The basic food fish for cold-water game fish are smelt and yellow perch, so any lure or fly that represents these baitfish is a sensible choice. Dardevles, Little Cleos, Krocodiles, Rapalas, and Rebels are popular lures; silver, blue and silver, orange and silver, green and silver, and gold are the standard lure finishes on Lake Champlain and should be in everyone's tackle box. Another very popular lure is the copper and silver Sutton spoon, which comes in many shapes and sizes. Multicolored flutter spoons, such as the Dardevle Flutter Chuck, Evil Eye, and Stinger, as well as Mooselooks, have been very popular and productive in recent years. If you come to Lake Champlain to cast for lake trout in the spring and fall, make sure you have a lot of red and white Dardevles and blue and silver Little Cleos in the ¼- to ¾-ounce sizes. They are among the most popular and most productive casting lures used on the lake. Even though I fish for all different species of cold-water and cool-water fish, in my opinion there is nothing quite like catching them on or near the surface. By using light tackle for surface fishing, you get at least twice the fight out of the fish as you would on heavy tackle in deep water.

Most people who troll for trout and salmon use spoons and minnow-imitating lures exclusively, but if you want to increase your success ratio, streamer flies are the answer. Whether you flatline or downrig, there are some days when using trolling flies could mean the difference between getting skunked or limiting out. When trolling in the spring and fall for trout and salmon, I use fly rods or ultralight spinning tackle with 4-pound leader or line with a number 3 or number 5 split shot about 18 inches up from the fly. Single or tandem flies in most smelt patterns will do. The most popular are the Grey Ghost, Green Ghost, Governor Akins, Joe's Smelt, Champlain

A rare catch. Brian Doyle caught this 10-pound female muskellunge at the mouth of the Great Chazy River. Muskies are uncommon in Lake Champlain.

Jane, and Nine Three, which are smelt patterns. The Mickey Finn and Edson Tiger, Golden Ghost, and Champlain Special are yellow patterns that, I believe, effectively represent the small perch that salmon and trout also feed on.

Night crawlers and smelt are the top natural live baits to use in Lake Champlain. Night crawlers and ground worms are cast out from the bank or boat and allowed to bounce along the bottom, just as would be done in any trout stream. When bottom fishing with smelt, use a whole uncleaned smelt, which will float. Thread an English Gorge hook through the smelt and weight it with a slip sinker and split shot so that the smelt will float about a foot or two from the bottom. When drift-fishing in a boat, use a whole gutted smelt, which will sink. Hook it through the mouth and put a sinker about a foot above it.

Use a whole gutted smelt for tip-up fishing, but hook the bait by the dorsal fin so it will hang straight.

Launching Areas

There are four major launching sites in the trout and salmon areas of the lake.

1. Point Au Roche Ramp, located a few miles north of Plattsburgh (exits 35 and 36 off the Northway, I-87)
2. Peru Dock, located a few miles south of Plattsburgh (exits 35 and 36 off the Northway)
3. Willsboro Bay Launch Area (exit 33 off the Northway)
4. Westport Launch Area (exit 30 off the Northway)

All these are excellent launching areas with good ramps for almost any size boat and plenty of room for parking.

Shore-Fishing Areas

Except for the state park areas on Point Au Roche and Ausable Point, most shore-fishing areas are owned by the local towns or are privately owned. Moving from north to south, these areas are:

1. Point Au Roche Park, located a few miles north of Plattsburgh (Northway exit 40)
2. The mouth of the Saranac River, located in downtown Plattsburgh (Northway exits 36 and 37)
3. Port Kent, cliff area just south of ferry landing (Northway exit 34)
4. Willsboro Point, privately owned point with public access (Northway exit 33)
5. Willsboro/Boquet River below Willsboro Dam (Northway exit 33)
6. Essex Town Park, just south of Ferry Landing (Northway exit 32)
7. Lachutte River Dam in Ticonderoga (Northway exits 28 and 29)

The Port Kent and Essex areas are mainly used by smelt fishermen. No bait-fishing is allowed on Willsboro Point. As mentioned above, most of these areas are not state owned, so these access areas can be taken away if we don't keep them neat and clean. They are strictly for fishing, so no camping or picnicking is allowed.

If you are fishing the Willsboro-Westport area, most accommodations and meals will be found right along NY 22. US 9 has a number of restaurants and motels from Keeseville to Plattsburgh, the latter being the North Country's big city, with many motels and restaurants. For a list of accommodations and eating establishments, contact the Plattsburgh–North Country Chamber of Commerce (518-563-1000; www.northcountrychamber.com) or the Ticonderoga Chamber of Commerce (518-585-6619; www.ticon derogany.com).

Fishing Seasons and Regulations

Lake Champlain's trout and salmon season is year-round, generally including the tributaries up to the first barrier. The size limit for lake trout and salmon is 15 inches; for browns and rainbows it's 12 inches. To fish the New York side, you'll need a New York license. New York and Vermont now have a reciprocal fishing license agreement whereby New Yorkers can fish the Vermont side of the main lake with just a New York fishing license. Fishing the inland sea in Vermont, however, requires a Vermont license. In any case, be sure to read the rules and regulations booklet that is issued with your New York State license. There is a specific section in the booklet on Lake Champlain.

Lake Champlain is probably the largest underfished lake in the country, and it offers variety that may not be matched anywhere. I believe the unique thing about Champlain's trout and salmon fishing is that you can fish for them a good six months of the year right on top—and isn't that the most enjoyable way of getting them?

About the Author

Peter Casamento is a full-time licensed Adirondack guide and owner of the Adirondack-Champlain Guide Service in Willsboro since 1978. Specializing in the Adirondacks and Lake Champlain, he and the numerous guides who work with him host more than two thousand sportspeople each year. Peter resides in Willsboro on Long Pond with his wife, Jane.

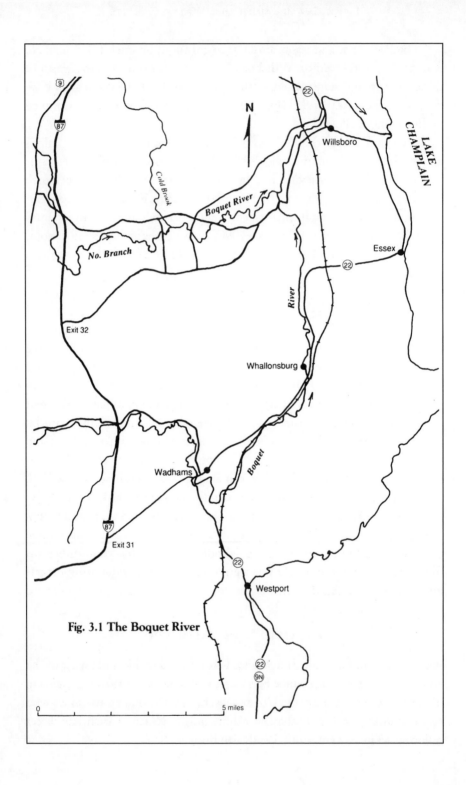

Fig. 3.1 The Boquet River

CHAPTER THREE

Salmon Fever!

Don Lee

M y introduction to landlocked salmon came in the late '70s while fishing for brown trout in the Saranac River below Imperial Mill Dam in the city of Plattsburgh. The pool below the dam is about 1 acre in size, and at that time a low head hydroelectric generating plant was in operation. The turbines spinning to produce electricity would discharge water at the bottom of the mill powerhouse. One evening while fly-fishing at the base of the dam, trying for the big browns, I was in for a nice surprise. My muddler minnow fly suddenly stopped and raced off across the pool, and then leaped in the air with a 4-pound landlocked Atlantic salmon attached. Having never caught one or even seen one other than in a sporting magazine, I was taken aback at first. After doing a little research, I soon figured out that my brown trout was, in fact, a nice salmon.

I kept my secret for a few weeks, but soon I ran into another fellow fishing the same area who had caught a salmon, too. Sam Thuesen was the other angler, and a lifelong friendship ensued. Sam told me that a third angler, Bruce Handley, the first president of the Lake Champlain Chapter of Trout Unlimited, was also having luck with salmon. Our secret lasted only that one season, and then many people discovered the exceptional landlocked Atlantic salmon fishing that was developing in the Saranac River. In the summer of 2009, as I write this chapter, there is renewed hope for the increased revitalization of this fishery.

Landlocked Atlantic Salmon: History and Restoration

Once found in nearly all of the major rivers of North America, between Connecticut and the Canadian Maritimes, Atlantic salmon are now found primarily in New Brunswick, Newfoundland, Labrador, Nova Scotia, and Quebec. Efforts to reestablish salmon runs in major American rivers in Maine and Connecticut have met with limited success. Atlantic salmon are anadromous in that as adults they migrate from the Atlantic Ocean to the cool, clear waters of North America rivers, sometimes traveling thousands of miles to reach suitable spawning habitat. Once deposited in their spawning rivers, salmon eggs will remain there from one to three years as hatchlings developing into small salmon before migrating back to the ocean as smolt. Adult salmon, after spawning, may winter over in the river, or some may return to the ocean that fall. Unlike Pacific salmon, which complete their life cycle and die after spawning, Atlantic salmon can spawn several times during their lifetime.

Landlocked salmon are exactly that, landlocked. After the ice ages and many geological changes, some man-made, salmon were cut off from reaching the ocean and became a subspecies, *Salmo salar sebago*. As many fishing biologists will tell you, it's the same fish! For our salmon, Lake Champlain becomes their ocean, and they adapt to feeding on smelt and other small fish in the lake. Pound for pound, they fight and exhibit many of the tendencies of their oceangoing cousins, and yes, they taste good, too.

The largest inland population of landlocks was in the Great Lakes, but by the early 1900s they were eliminated or nearly so by human destruction of the watersheds due to pollution. Lake Champlain landlocks were extirpated in the late 1800s due primarily to the erection of dams, which blocked access to necessary spawning habitat and eliminated natural reproduction. But today, nearly 30 years after reintroducing landlocked Atlantic salmon to several waters in the Adirondacks, we find fisheries improving, but not without some major setbacks.

The Great Lakes Atlantic salmon restoration has met numerous setbacks due to the infestation of sea lamprey, a parasite fish that, when mature, attaches to salmonids and bores a hole into the cavity of the host fish, sucking out bodily fluids until the fish dies. They spawn in rivers much like salmon and are prolific, reproducing thousands from a single pair. Unfortunately, sea lamprey have also found their way into Lake Champlain, wreaking havoc with the salmon program. Although a major setback to the landlock restoration programs in the Great Lakes and Lake Champlain, fishery biologists were able to develop a lampricide that kills the ammocoetes (young lamprey offspring) in the rivers and river deltas. Today, with the help from state and federal governments (in the United States and Canada), ongoing treatment programs with lampricide are bringing this predator back into controllable numbers. Landlocked salmon populations are steadily increasing, along with some natural reproduction. In August 2009, for the first time in more than a century, scientists found wild-born Atlantic salmon in the Salmon River, a Lake Ontario tributary that once teemed with fish, suggesting that the native species is recovering after many years of reproductive failure there. This failure to reproduce in the Great Lakes was caused by the presence of another nonnative species, the alewife, which got into the lakes more than 50 years ago through canals and the St. Lawrence Seaway. Slightly smaller than smelt, alewives compete directly with them for zooplankton and microscopic crustaceans. Alewives impact landlocked salmon by causing a thiamine deficiency when salmon primarily feed on them. When landlocked salmon reproduce, the hatchlings soon die of thiamine deficiency. The solution in the Great Lakes was accidental: Pacific salmon were introduced to control the burgeoning population of alewives, which would periodically die off fowling beaches and shoreline. Once the population of alewives was diminished by predation, natural reproduction by landlocked Atlantic salmon started to occur again. Alewives were recently discovered in Lake Champlain and have yet to impact natural reproduction of its salmon, but it will have to be monitored closely over the next few years.

The major concentration of landlocked salmon in northern New York continues to be Lake Champlain and its major New York tributaries: the Ausable, Boquet, and Saranac rivers. All three rivers find their source high in the Adirondack mountains and flow more than 30 miles before they reach Lake Champlain. Cool, clear, and clean, they are three of the greatest coldwater fisheries in New York State and maybe the whole Northeast.

In the 1950s, Atlantic salmon were reintroduced into the Boquet River system once more. Encouraging results led to a full-scale restoration project in 1973. By the spring of 1976, many adult salmon started showing up below the Willsboro dam, and fishing was reported as excellent. A major setback occurred with sea lamprey populations exploding and causing heavy predation on trout and salmon. An experimental lamprey-control program started in 1990 proved successful and has been formally adopted by Quebec, New York, and Vermont. It was recently reported by U.S. Fish and Wildlife that this long-term maintenance program is producing good results in reducing sea lamprey populations. We now hope for significant and continued improvement to the landlocked salmon fishery.

When, Where, and How to Fish for Landlocked Atlantic Salmon

The questions always come up about when, where, and how to fish for landlocked Atlantic salmon. The "when" is primarily in the spring and fall of the year. The spring run is commonly called a false run. Salmon come into the rivers in springtime shortly after ice-out and the first spring thaw, which usually happens in late March or early April. Salmon aren't coming into the river to spawn, but rather to feed. With the warmer spring days, rivers warm up faster than the lakes where our landlocks live. At this time, smelt, shiners, and dace come into the warmer waters of the rivers to spawn. These small fish just happen to be the primary food source for the landlocked salmon, hence the food fest begins. Spring salmon are easier to catch because they are actively feeding and can be easily caught on worms, lures, and flies. The spring run usually lasts until late May or early June, but it seems to end once river water temperatures hit 60 degrees Fahrenheit.

Spring salmon are like teenagers; they have lots of energy and are everywhere! They average a little over 18 inches and weigh 2½ to 3 pounds, and they are really fun to catch. Beware though, because each spring a few larger fish (5 to 10 pounds) are hooked, and they will really test your tackle and skills.

The fall run is the true spawning run, and salmon at this time are primarily interested in procreating. In fall, when they enter the rivers, it's all about finding a mate and suitable spawning habitat (cobble and water flows) that will keep their eggs alive and safe. Males usually enter the rivers first, around late August or early September, depending on water conditions. It's usually that first cool night after a heavy rain that decides the beginning of the run. Females tend to follow about a week or two later. Actual spawning occurs the end of October or first week of November. Fall fish are usually larger and fewer in numbers than the spring run.

A mixed catch of landlocks and steelhead from the Boquet.

Having fished for both Atlantic salmon and landlocked Atlantic salmon, I can tell you that other than the flies used to fish for them, the rods, reels, lines, and leaders are all the same. I'll start with traditional methods for fishing for Atlantic salmon, considered the fish of a thousand casts, especially in the fall. Fish that have just come into the river are called "bright" fish or "chromers" because they are silvery and shiny. These salmon are easier to catch and will take a fly or lure much quicker than a dark salmon. A "dark salmon" is usually one that has been in the river a week or two, and whose body has started to darken up to match the coloration of the river bottom. It's nature's way of adding a little camouflage to protect the species. Spring fish are almost always bright and shiny, with the exception of a slink salmon. A slink salmon is one that spawned in the fall, wintered over in the river, and does not migrate back to the lake/ocean until spring. They will usually hang around the mouth of the river, feeding and gaining strength prior to entering the lake/ocean. They retain their dark color until they're back in the lake.

Fly-fishing for salmon is usually done with 6 to 9 weight rods 8½ to 10 feet in length. Longer rods from 9 to 10 feet seem to work best for line management and false casting. Today we are even seeing a resurgence in two-handed spey rods. They cast great distances and can cover more water, especially when you are wading. They are sometimes helpful if you have a bum shoulder, too. You don't mention salmon fishing without mentioning persistence and patience: you have to keep your fly in the water if you want to catch one! A good single-action reel that has a line capacity for your fly line plus 200 yards of backing (20- to 30-pound test) is a must. Most new reels have a smooth rim that can be palmed for extra breaking on that "big one." A couple hundred yards of backing is sometimes necessary to allow the fish to run a little, slowly tire, and become easier to land. Landing a salmon can be safely done by tailing. Unlike most fish, a salmon's tailfin is hard and splayed out, and will not collapse like a trout fin. This allows the angler to lead the fish within reaching distance and slip a hand around the tail, thus capturing the fish. I strongly recommend this method of landing a salmon, especially if you are going to release it. A fishing buddy helping you do this can make the catching experience memorable for both of you. I also recommend pinching the barbs down on all hooks for a couple of reasons. The first is safety. If you fly-fish, you will get nicked by a hook. If the barb is pinched down, it might still smart, but usually no emergency room visit is necessary. Back it out, put antiseptic on the wound, and continue fishing. Second, the release of the salmon will be easier. With no barbs, the hook can safely be removed from the salmon without causing injury. Also, on large salmon, with the traditional down and across cast, the fish is almost always hooked in the corner of the jaw. A barbless hook will penetrate better for a good hook-up and maybe the catch of a lifetime.

A good pair of polarized glasses is a must. Remember, you only have two eyes, and fish hooks flying through the air with a few feathers attached can seriously injure them. Always wear eye protection when fishing. The polarized glasses also help you to see river structure when wading, preventing unnecessary slips, falls, and dunks.

If I had one fly line to get, it would be a floating line. It presents the fly at the right depth, normally the surface down to about 6 inches. The majority of all salmon are caught in this range. Spate or high-water conditions sometimes require the use of sinking or sink-tip lines to get down to the fish. To always be prepared, you can get a new line called a multi-tip fly line, which has a running line with interchangeable tips, from floating to sinking, at various speeds and depths. I have a couple; they work great and are easy to cast.

Leaders should be tapered and about 7 to 9 feet in length. Under most conditions Atlantic salmon are not leader shy. Low-water conditions may dictate going lighter and longer. For local rivers, leaders should be tipped out with 2X 9-pound test. For the oceangoing cousins, OX 15-pound test is sometimes required. Remember to always check your terminal tackle. Many anglers have lost nice fish due to wind knots, line abrasions, or faulty knots. You will be doing a lot of casting, and a back cast is bound to accidentally hit the shingle, causing a broken hook point. Check your fly and hook point often to prevent a lost fish.

The "where" part of the salmon fishing question is Lake Champlain and its major tributaries. The Boquet River, located about 30 miles south of Plattsburgh, in the town of Willsboro in Essex County, is where our present-day landlocked fishing got started nearly 40 years ago. With a fish ladder built in 1980, salmon fishing is available 12 miles upriver as far as Wadhams Falls. Fishing access is good both above and below the Willsboro dam and fish ladder. The best fishing is the big pool 200 yards below the fish ladder. It's also a great viewing spot for anglers and tourists to watch the salmon and the fishing. Access to the mouth of the river and Lake Champlain is also available with small boats. A word of caution: you may be somewhat protected in the river, but if you venture any distance from shore on the broad lake, watch the winds and weather. They can change in a hurry, possibly putting anglers and boaters in danger! Besides the spring and fall runs, after major rainstorms the Boquet will have small summer runs of salmon coming no farther than the fish ladder. With good parking, access, and fishing, the Boquet is well worth it.

Coming back north, the next major tributary is the Ausable River. It has extremely limited fishing access. Salmon can only go as far upstream as the impassable falls at Ausable Chasm. This limits any major spawning activity. Also, most of the land above the US 9 bridge is private. The best fishing is at or just above the bridge itself. Boat access is available, but check fishing regulations. It's still worth a try, though; nice trout and salmon are caught there spring and fall.

Lastly, we come to the Saranac River, in the city of Plattsburgh in Clinton County. Salmon were once so important to the local populace that a salmon graces the seal of Clinton County. It has been historically documented that before the dams blocked the annual fall spawning migration, farmers in Morrisonville (approximately 10 miles from Lake Champlain) would take horse and wagons into the river, loading them with salmon weighing as much as 20 pounds in an hour's time. One can only wonder what that salmon run must have been like. Today, many years later, we again have a salmon run, but it only goes as far as Imperial Mill Dam, located behind Plattsburgh State University. With a new fish ladder already installed at Treadwell Mills (a dam 1 mile upriver), one wonders why a ladder or dam removal hasn't occurred at Imperial Mill. It's the last major barrier preventing salmon from reaching their historic spawning habitat below Kent Falls, always a natural barrier to the salmon. The effort continues today to remove the barrier to salmon. One can only hope!

The Saranac River, as it does exist, is still a great river for trout and salmon in the spring and fall. Most spring fishing is done from the Kennedy Bridge downstream of the mouth of the river. Wading access from the right bank looking downstream is good, but it must be explored in the springtime to check for changes to the river bottom caused by ice damming in the area. For anglers who are wading, a wading staff can at times be a lifesaver. I strongly recommend one in all three rivers discussed. On the left bank, or monument side, of the river, a wall with a parallel sidewalk makes access very easy. There is also a handicapped-accessible fishing platform in front of the Ticonderoga Monument that extends 8 feet out over the river. It's a good spot, and it does get used with good results. Just downstream of the CP Railroad Bridge is a footbridge across the river that also provides good fishing access. Fly fishermen typically fish below the footbridge on a gravel bar that extends along the right side of the river. Many spring and fall salmon are caught here. Do not attempt to fish from or cross the railroad bridge—it's dangerous and illegal. A small boat ramp is also available across from the Municipal Lighting Department. A new launch at Wilcox Dock is available

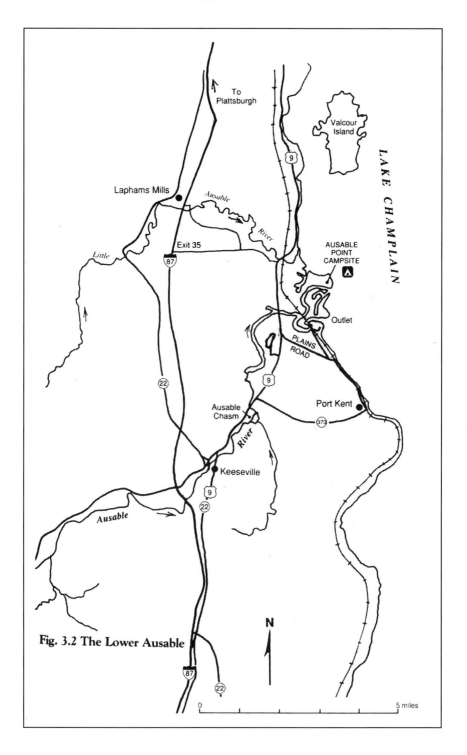

Fig. 3.2 The Lower Ausable

for larger boats. Anglers fishing from the boats use spoons, trolling flies, and worms to catch salmon. Planer boards and downriggers have also been used with great success by the boaters.

Fly fishermen seem to have the best luck using Black Ghost, Grey Ghost, and other smelt-imitating streamer patterns. Most takes seem to come as the fly is swinging and starting to rise to the surface when your fly line straightens out downstream. Remember, you don't have to strike hard; just lift your rod tip and keep a tight line, and then hang on for the fight of a lifetime. Salmon fishing, no matter what angling method you use, is fun.

Remember angling ethics, and when other anglers are present, rotate pools and good fishing spots. This allows everyone to fish the whole pool. Also, remember to check the fishing regulations for the time of year and area you are fishing. These regulations change from time to time.

Other areas to fish for landlocked Atlantic salmon are: Lake George, Schroon Lake, Schroon River, Upper Saranac Lake, Upper Chateaugay Lake, and Indian Lake. All offer good landlocked fishing.

For more information on Adirondack salmon fishing, contact the Department of Environmental Conservation (DEC) in Ray Brook (518-897-1200) for the latest list of waters stocked with landlocked salmon and open to fishing. New water is stocked from time to time, and the DEC lists will keep you up-to-date. By the way, some of the smaller salmon lakes offer great fishing just after ice-out and provide an accommodating setting for the angler with a small boat.

About the Author

Don Lee is a longtime sportsman with a passion for fishing for Atlantic salmon. A charter member and past president of the Lake Champlain Chapter of Trout Unlimited, he has mentored hundreds of elementary students on the environment through the Adopt a Salmon program. The program includes raising salmon from eggs to fry in school classrooms and then stocking them in Lake Champlain tributaries, using the life cycle of the Atlantic salmon as a tool to teach about the value of clean watersheds and the environment. He lives in Morrisonville, New York, on the banks of the Saranac River, and he is always available to help others learn the finer techniques of salmon fishing.

CHAPTER FOUR

The Mighty Saranac

John Spissinger

F orget about what you think you're going to catch when you cast
into the waters of New York's mighty Saranac River. Ply a small
streamer for browns and rainbows in the deep turbulent pockets of
the South Branch, and your fly might be ravaged by a hungry, deep-bodied
smallmouth or by an angry northern pike. Troll slowly, or perhaps cast a jig
for walleye in Union Falls Pond, and you might have to brace yourself for the
dogged, powerful runs of a heavy, lake-reared brown trout. Lob a night
crawler into the smooth currents at the mouth of the river in the city of
Plattsburgh, and you just might be treated to the dazzling acrobatics of a
fresh-run steelhead or landlocked salmon. Clearly, the rule of thumb to
follow when fishing the mighty Saranac is "expect the unexpected."

The Saranac may be unique among Adirondack rivers in terms of the
varied opportunities it presents to angling enthusiasts. Not only does it hold
an interesting blend of cool- and cold-water game fish, it also affords very
different types of water that can be fished in different ways according to the
individual preferences and skills of the angler. There is plenty of good water
to suit the desires of spin, fly, and bait fishermen alike. Public access is excellent throughout the 65-mile stretch of river from Saranac Lake to Plattsburgh. Much of the river is navigable and can be fished from a canoe or small
boat. Additionally, there is ample access for wading or bank fishing.

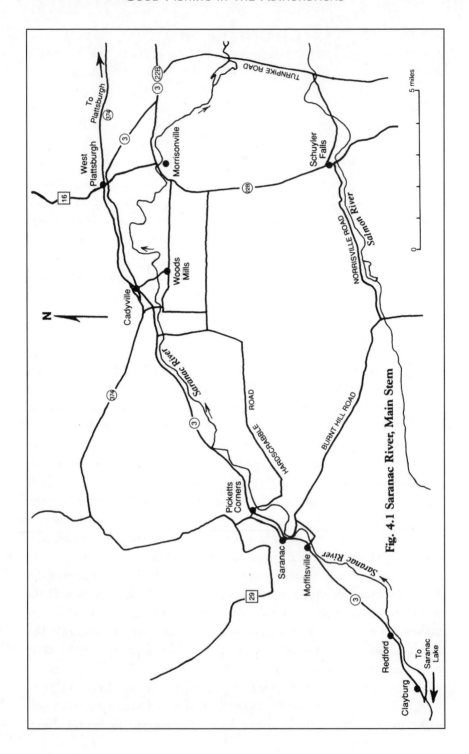

Fig. 4.1 Saranac River, Main Stem

Although there are a few seasonal hot spots where anglers tend to congregate, there's enough quality water spread throughout the river to ensure the peace and solitude that many anglers cherish. Combine these features, and you have a river that has something to offer every angler.

Overview

Located in the northeastern sector of New York's Adirondack Mountains, the Saranac flows easterly through parts of Franklin, Essex, and Clinton counties. Less heralded than its neighbor, the Ausable, the geography of the Saranac has much in common with that other great trout river. The headwaters of the Saranac and Ausable lie but a few miles apart in the High Peaks region of the Adirondack Park. The main stems of both rivers are formed by the confluence of their two branches: the East and West branches of the Ausable, and the North and South branches of the Saranac. With Lake Champlain their eventual destination, the rivers traverse roughly parallel courses before entering the lake fewer than 10 miles apart.

Unlike the Ausable, the Saranac's fishing has been decisively impacted by hydroelectric development. More than any other factor, the several hydroelectric impoundments along the Saranac account for the variety, abundance, and local intermingling of cold-, cool-, and warm-water species of fish. Anglers and environmentalists throughout the country have been rightfully concerned about the detrimental effects of such projects. Frequently, habitat is severely altered or destroyed, and some species of fish are totally eradicated. Occasionally, though, hydro projects have actually had a positive impact on fishery resources by creating or improving habitat. Arguably, the Saranac is one of those watersheds that has benefited from its hydro impoundments. Supporting this contention are the fine walleye and smallmouth populations that have developed behind some of its dams and the establishment of very good brown trout fisheries in the tailwaters below the dams, particularly below the Kent Falls dam. Presently, there are nine hydro projects on the Saranac. From a recreational standpoint, the best fishing opportunities are found at Franklin Falls and Union Falls ponds on the South Branch and in the waters above the Kent Falls, Mill C, and Cadyville dams on the main stem. Some of the most varied fishing on the Saranac system takes place in the waters above these dams.

Franklin Falls and Union Falls flows or impoundments are both rather sizable bodies of water. Franklin Falls Pond spreads over 435 acres and has a

KATHY APRILL

The Saranac offers great fly-fishing opportunities.

maximum depth of 30 feet. Larger still, Union Falls Pond encompasses 1,575 acres but is slightly shallower at 20 feet. Both ponds are classified as warm-water fisheries by the Department of Environmental Conservation (DEC). An excellent walleye fishery exists in Union Falls Pond, which is stocked heavily with this species. The walleyes are not large, but they are plentiful. Occasional fish are taken in the 6- to 8-pound range. Franklin Falls Pond also supports an increasingly productive walleye fishery with excellent catches reported in recent years. In addition to walleye, northern pike are prevalent in both ponds. Again, while the fish are not huge, they are abundant and provide excellent sport. Fish in the 10- to 12-pound range have been taken, and there are probably some larger specimens lurking in the depths. Smallmouth are also present in good numbers, and there are enough 3- to 5-pounders around to keep things interesting. You would not want to fish either Franklin Falls or Union Falls pond if brown trout were your primary quarry. Each year, however, both ponds surrender some very large browns that take up residence in the still waters. Besides the game fish, yellow perch, bullhead, and other panfish provide both action and excellent table fare. A few of the perch grow to a foot or more, and during the winter they, along with the walleye and northerns, attract a popular following of ice fishermen.

Getting to Franklin Falls or Union Falls pond is relatively easy. The River Road in Bloomingdale, the Cold Brook Road in Vermontville, and the Alder Brook Road at the junction of County Route 26 all lead into the area from the south side of NY 3. Yet another route to take, especially if you've been fishing the Ausable, is to drive north on the Silver Lake Road in Ausable Forks to the Union Falls Road near Silver Lake.

While private camps dot the shorelines of both ponds, there are plenty of places to fish once there. At Franklin Falls, there are several roadside pull-offs and paths that lead down to the shoreline. Although there are no trailer launch sites, it is quite easy to get into the pond with a canoe or small car-top boat, especially near the dam. Similar access is available on Union Falls Pond. In addition, there is a private launch site and boat livery near the end of the impoundment. If you fish Franklin Falls, don't neglect the deep, slow-water stretch below the dam. Sometimes the walleye, northern, and small-mouth fishing here is as good as on the main lake. However, caution should be used when fishing along the steep ledges and rocks above the gorge. Similarly, it is also prudent to be cautious when boating in Union Falls and Franklin Falls as there are boulders and stumps throughout these impoundments. It's a good idea to speak with fellow anglers or to seek the advice of the proprietor of the launch on Union Falls to learn where the channels and hazards lie, as well as where the seasonal hot spots are.

Fishing on the Lower Saranac

The fishing opportunities above the three dams on the lower Saranac, near Cadyville, are similar to those described at Franklin Falls and Union Falls ponds. Here, though, smallmouth attract the most attention, while northerns and walleye play a somewhat lesser role. The reservoirs above the Kent Falls and Mill C dams are quite narrow, at most a few hundred yards wide, and short, about ½ mile long. Behind the Cadyville dam the river is backed up for several miles, although it remains narrow.

Because the Cadyville, Mill C, and Kent Falls dams are not more than 2 miles apart, it's easy to sample the fishing at each spot on a single day. NY 3 passes alongside the Cadyville reservoir, and intersections with the Harvey Bridge and Goddeau roads provide access to the Mill C and Kent Falls reservoirs. The New York State Electric and Gas Company (NYSEG) maintains parking areas on both waters. It is possible to put in a canoe or small car-top boat at these sites, though most of the fishing is done from the shore. The village of Cadyville maintains a small recreational area, including a trailer launch facility, right off NY 3. While parking is limited by the size of this facility, it remains a popular access site. Between Cadyville and Saranac, about 7 miles upstream, there are several intersecting roads that provide additional access. Some local anglers like to float this stretch, launching their canoes at the Hardscrabble Road bridge in Saranac and drifting downstream to the Cadyville beach, where a second car is left.

Trout Fishing

The Saranac's reputation as a blue-ribbon trout river is borne out in the productive pools, riffles, and pocket water above and below the several impoundments. Trout fishing enthusiasts can easily explore and sample these stretches by taking a leisurely drive along NY 3, starting either in Plattsburgh or in Saranac Lake. About one-third of the South Branch, half of the North Branch, and virtually all of the main stem border this highway. There are many parking areas along the river that allow you to make close-up inspections of promising stretches of water. Moreover, additional information can be gleaned from local sources, like the bait and tackle shops, small grocery stores, inns, and campgrounds that are evident along NY 3. Assuming that you're leaving from Saranac Lake, the following paragraphs should give a picture of what to look for as you head downstream.

From the Lake Flower dam to the hamlet of Bloomingdale, the South Branch wanders through meadows and swampland. Road access is relatively limited along this slow, deep run, and floating it by canoe is probably the best approach. Although a few trout are stocked in the village of Saranac Lake on a put-and-take basis, smallmouth and northerns are more numerous. Just before Bloomingdale, the river veers away from NY 3 and quickens its tempo as it flows through pine and hardwood forests. Good access is found along the River Road in Bloomingdale, which follows the river downstream to Franklin Falls Pond. Generally, the faster slicks and pocket water hold brown and rainbow trout, while a mixed bag is to be found in the slower pools and runs. After passing through Franklin Falls and Union Falls ponds, the South Branch resumes its course and is largely inaccessible until it crosses the Silver Lake Road bridge. The river is heavily posted and patrolled on both sides of the bridge, but there are three public fishing/parking areas just north of the bridge down to the junction with NY 3 in Clayburg. Anglers must descend steep banks to get to the river from these sites, but there is excellent brown and rainbow fishing in the turbulent boulder-strewn pocket water. Catch-and-release regulations govern a part of this stretch, approximately 100 yards above the confluence with the North Branch upstream 1.4 miles to Stord Brook.

For the beauty, solitude, and enchantment that so many anglers feel to be the essence of trout fishing, few Adirondack rivers can match the charms of the Saranac's North Branch. It is a cold, quiet little river from its headwaters to its junction with the brawling South Branch in Clayburg. Dense, overhanging alders; waist-deep oxbow bends; and undercut banks provide ideal cover for the brook, brown, and rainbow trout that thrive in its waters. The river is easy to get to from several well-maintained public parking areas on NY 3, from Clayburg 5 miles upstream to Alder Brook. During May and June, this stretch sees some moderate to heavy angling pressure. Yet few anglers bother to fish the headwaters of the North Branch, which can be reached via the Goldsmith Road (which joins NY 3 a few miles west of Alder Brook). The river is much smaller here, in places no more than a few feet wide, and thickly forested. Native brookies are small but plentiful, and occasional wild browns are an added bonus. Although there are a number of private camps and posted property along the Goldsmith Road, the DEC has secured public fishing rights in various spots. The fish are highly selective on the North Branch, and often you have to work hard to catch them. Still, there are few places anywhere in the region that look as intriguing as the North Branch of the Saranac.

Reasonably good trout water continues on the main stem of the river from Clayburg to Saranac, 6 miles downstream. Because the river is so broad and shallow here, it doesn't appear to be a productive reach of water. However, the choppy riffles disguise deeper subsurface trenches and pockets. Trout hold in these protected areas and migrate to feed along the shallower edges. Although it takes practice to learn how to read this water, some surprisingly good fishing can be had. Several riverside parking areas are present along this stretch. Generally, the Hardscrabble Road bridge in Saranac marks the dividing line between cold- and cool-water species. Shortly below the bridge the effects of the Cadyville dam are evident, and smallmouth, northerns, walleye, and panfish displace the trout.

The final stretch of trout water worth mentioning on the Saranac lies between the Kent Falls dam downstream to the Clinton County Fairgrounds. Catch-and-release regulations apply to the section from the Millstone Monument in the village of Morrisonville upstream to the Kent Falls dam.

Although periodic releases below the Kent Falls dam can affect water levels, recently instituted "run of river" operations have tended to stabilize flows and prevent wild fluctuations in the river. Still, the swift currents and loose cobble bottom combine to make wading both tricky and challenging. The Kent Falls Road borders the river from NY 22B in Morrisonville upstream to the dam. NYSEG maintains a fishermen's parking area below the powerhouse, and some roadside pull-offs give access farther downstream.

Best Seasons to Fish

Because the Saranac is such a large and varied river, the best time of year to fish it pretty much depends on what you hope to catch and where you plan to go. June and September are probably the best months for both cool- and cold-water species. Although trout season remains open on a year-round basis, the action is usually better on the lower sections of the main stem in late April and early May, and then improves upstream as the waters warm. During the hottest days of summer, the North Branch, with its shaded waters and many spring seepages, is a good bet. Walleye and northern pike fishing above the dams is best right after the season opens in mid-May through June, and then again in the fall. Not to be forgotten is the occasionally excellent ice fishing on Union Falls Pond in February. Smallmouth fishing remains consistently good from opening day in June through October. (New regulations permit bass fishing on a catch-and-release basis from December 1 thru the Friday preceding the second Saturday in June.)

Fishing Tips

If the fish are in a cooperative mood, the flies, lures, and baits that work well for the different species elsewhere are also usually productive on the Saranac. Worms provide the most action as there's not a fish in the river that won't gobble one up from time to time. Live or salted minnows will reduce the number of strikes by nuisance fish like river chubs and improve chances for a good-sized northern, walleye, smallmouth, or brown. Small jigs, spinnerbaits, plugs, and crankbaits also work well for these species. Fly fishermen will encounter many of the major eastern mayfly hatches starting with the hendricksons in early to mid-May. The green drake hatch, which begins in early June on the lower river and moves upstream in successive weeks, can be phenomenal. Actually, some of the best smallmouth fishing occurs when this fly

*A view of the often tumbling Saranac River, below the rapids at Redford.
This young angler will be tested by the heavy water.*

is on the water above the dams. Trout will often ignore these juicy morsels
and instead feed heavily on smaller caddis flies. But smallmouth find the
drakes irresistible and will smash them with a vengeance. Large stone fly
nymphs are productive in the South Branch's pocket water, while terrestrial
imitations and midges pay off on the North Branch in summer. As searching
patterns, the traditional Adams, Muddler, Hare's Ear nymphs, Ausable
Wulffs, and some elk-hair caddis tied in various colors and sizes will be useful
in most situations. With fly patterns, as with lures and baits, it's always prudent to compare notes with fellow anglers to learn what seems to be the hot
pick at any given time.

Landlocked Salmon

Although the city of Plattsburgh marks the end of the Saranac's journey toward Lake Champlain, the lower section of the river contains yet another exciting dimension of its diverse fishery. In the 1960s, the New York DEC began experimental stockings of landlocked salmon in Lake Champlain's major tributaries. Historical records indicate that salmon were once native to the lake, but pollution, overharvesting, and destruction of spawning habitat led to their demise by the mid-19th century. Results of the initial restorative stockings were encouraging as the salmon thrived on the abundant forage base in the lake and then returned to spawn in the lower reaches of the tributaries. Unfortunately, lamprey eel predation took a heavy toll on the salmon and lake trout. New York and Vermont instituted an experimental sea lamprey control program in the 1990s and have subsequently added Quebec to the effort, implementing the program on a permanent lake-wide basis. Salmon and trout populations are expected to increase as a result. In addition to lamprey control, hopes remain for the eventual construction of a fish ladder or removal of the Imperial Mill dam in the city of Plattsburgh. This would open up 10 additional miles of river for the fish and afford increased access for anglers. Presently, the Saranac supports a modest run of salmon during the spring and again in the fall as the fish move in to spawn.

The Saranac's spring salmon run usually begins in early April and continues through mid-May, depending on the water temperature and level. The best fishing occurs from the river's mouth to perhaps a half mile upstream. Although not particularly large at this time of year, averaging between 16 and 20 inches, the salmon are voracious feeders and will hit worms, spoons, plugs, streamers, nymphs, and even dry flies. More important than what to use is the task of getting your lure, bait, or fly down near the bottom in the swift, heavy waters. Fly-fishing anglers should come equipped with at least a 7-weight rod system and either a full-sinking or fast-sink-tip line. Spin and bait fishermen would do well to use a long, sturdy rod and reel with a dependable drag. Six- to 8-pound test line will normally handle the most challenging fish.

Early September marks the beginning of the fall spawning migration, with the peak coming by mid-October. The salmon ascend the river as far as the Imperial Mill dam, 3 miles upstream. The fish are both larger and more temperamental than in the spring because they are not actively feeding. Patience, in the form of repetitive casts into likely pools and runs, is the only

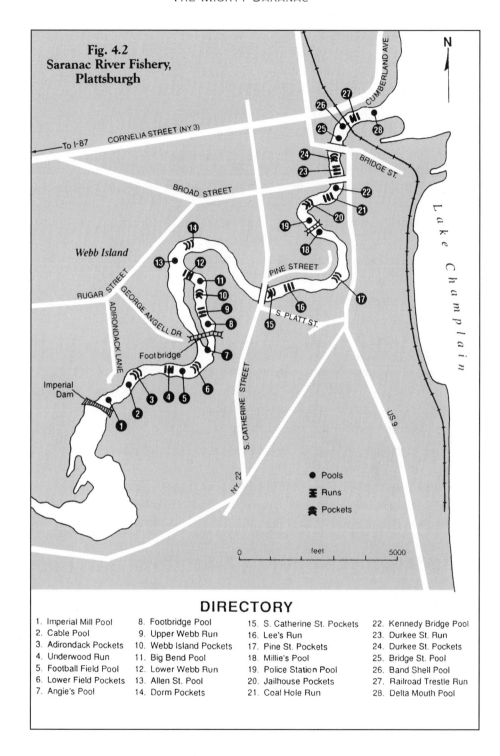

Fig. 4.2
Saranac River Fishery,
Plattsburgh

DIRECTORY

1. Imperial Mill Pool	8. Footbridge Pool	15. S. Catherine St. Pockets	22. Kennedy Bridge Pool
2. Cable Pool	9. Upper Webb Run	16. Lee's Run	23. Durkee St. Run
3. Adirondack Pockets	10. Webb Island Pockets	17. Pine St. Pockets	24. Durkee St. Pockets
4. Underwood Run	11. Big Bend Pool	18. Millie's Pool	25. Bridge St. Pool
5. Football Field Pool	12. Lower Webb Run	19. Police Station Pool	26. Band Shell Pool
6. Lower Field Pockets	13. Allen St. Pool	20. Jailhouse Pockets	27. Railroad Trestle Run
7. Angie's Pool	14. Dorm Pockets	21. Coal Hole Run	28. Delta Mouth Pool

sure way to maximize chances for success. When the salmon are inclined to hit, they will strike almost anything. Worms and plugs continue to work, although fly-fishing is perhaps more successful in fall. Some anglers have luck using traditional Atlantic salmon flies, with the Cosseboom and Rusty Rat being notable favorites. The majority of fly-fishing enthusiasts use streamers and bucktails. Yellow maribou streamers, Grey Ghosts, and Muddlers, in sizes 2 to 8, are popular patterns. Again, however, the exact pattern seems less important than the mood of the fish at any given moment.

With the lower river flowing directly through the city of Plattsburgh, fishing access is relatively easy. Following NY 3 or US 9 into the downtown section will lead to the mouth of the river. A small trailer launch facility can be found near the city's municipal treatment plant. A larger, more modern boat launch has been built at Wilcox Dock just north of the mouth on Cumberland Avenue. Ample parking is available at both sites, and there is access for handicapped anglers on the north bank above the footbridge. Access to the Imperial Mill Pool and to other productive stretches upstream is gained either by parking in back of the college fieldhouse and walking down to the river or by taking George Angell Drive to the footbridge in back of Plattsburgh High School. Both are located off Rugar Street near the SUNY Plattsburgh campus. Although fishing pressure can be concentrated and congested at times, rotating through popular pools and runs has become an increasingly common practice. In this respect the Saranac offers a qualitatively different angling experience more akin to traditional Atlantic salmon fishing.

For all the excitement that surrounds the Saranac's salmon run, anglers should still never be too sure about what they'll catch when they give it a try. Steelhead, smallmouth, walleye, northerns, brown trout, and even lakers swim in the same water as the migrant landlocks. And they hit just often enough to remind everyone of the truth of the proposition that when fishing the mighty Saranac, it's always best to "expect the unexpected"!

About the Author

Now retired, John Spissinger spends his abundant free time chasing trout, salmon, bowfin, steelhead, and carp in the Lake Champlain valley, and Atlantic salmon, mackerel, and sea trout on Cape Breton Island in Nova Scotia. An ardent fly-tier, John has taught fly-tying classes for nearly three decades through the Lake Champlain Chapter of Trout Unlimited. He lives in Peru, New York.

CHAPTER FIVE

The Legendary Ausable

Francis Betters

A book on fishing in the Adirondacks must include a chapter on the fabled West Branch of the Ausable River, which emanates from the highest peaks in the Adirondacks and, after joining the river's other main branch, flows eventually into Lake Champlain. The 30-mile-long West Branch is considered by many top outdoor writers and a multitude of anglers who have visited it to be one of the best trout streams in the East. Man, with all his wisdom and technical skill, could not have drawn a better blueprint for the perfect trout stream than Mother Nature has provided in the West Branch of the Ausable.

The West Branch

The Ausable River consists of two main branches, but it is the West Branch that has received the most attention, and rightfully so. The scenic beauty of its tumbling currents in the shadow of Whiteface Mountain, its clean unpolluted waters, and its abundance of trout make the West Branch a stream you will want to return to many times. It is this branch to which thousands of

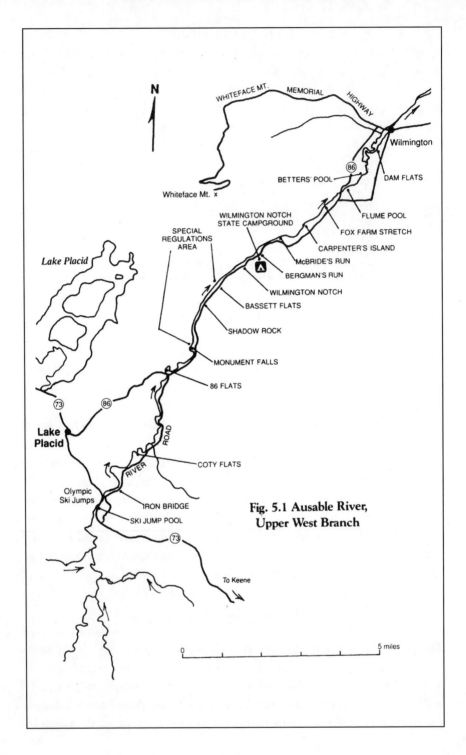

Fig. 5.1 Ausable River, Upper West Branch

fly and spin fishermen from all over the United States and many foreign countries come to try their luck at hooking one of the lunker brown trout that inhabit the many deep pools found here.

To understand why the West Branch is so good, it is important to know what ingredients go into producing a premier trout stream. This in turn necessitates knowing what the trout's requirements are—that is, what it takes to ensure an abundant and healthy population of fish. To sum these requirements up briefly: (1) unpolluted water, (2) a proper temperature range and a good supply of oxygen, (3) a plentiful food supply, and (4) cover.

How does the West Branch stack up in each of these four categories?

The water is still very clean in spite of increasing development in the area, and there are no great pollution problems menacing the river. The rich mineral water from the mountain feeder streams and the rich soil that is found along parts of the West Branch provide a good foundation for the food chain that eventually feeds the trout. The river provides good nourishment for both of the major sources of food the trout feed on, namely insects and baitfish.

Traversing a very cold part of the Adirondacks, the West Branch usually runs in a favorable temperature range for the trout. The shady conditions brought on by steep gorges and overhanging foliage help out in this regard, so that even in summer, the West Branch is often surprisingly chilly. As for the oxygen content, it is very good, thanks in part to the steep gradient. An abundant supply of oxygen is infused into the river as the water tumbles over the millions of rocks and boulders that make up the stream bottom in a large part of the West Branch.

The lower forms of life that the trout feed on are found in large numbers. The Ausable has an abundance of all three of the most important species of insects: mayflies, stone flies, and caddis flies. These insects are a good source of protein, and their abundance promotes good trout growth.

Finally, in terms of cover, the West Branch is hard to beat. Not only are there many deep pools, but there are a multitude of hiding and holding spots created by rocks and boulders and, in places, undercut banks.

It might be added here that another virtue of the Ausable is its very remoteness. It is far from any of the major cities of the east, and this has so far prevented overuse. Also, it is one of the most heavily stocked rivers in New York State.

The West Branch begins its fetal stage in the mountains. The headwaters comprise several brooks that flow essentially north from the Mount Marcy High Peaks area. As these tumbling mountain brooks converge, they gather

A happy angler.

strength, and at the junction of March Brook and South Meadow Brook, the West Branch is officially born. This is at the western edge of the South Meadows area and just south of the village of Lake Placid. The West Branch then winds its way down past the Olympic ski jumps just outside Lake Placid, picking up Indian Pass Brook on the way.

For the next 4 or 5 miles, the river is fairly calm as it makes its way through more meadowland, picking up a number of other small feeder streams. This is the part I refer to as the "Sweetwater" section of the Ausable. The river continues to grow, reaching the NY 86 bridge about 3 miles north of Lake Placid. After this crossing, the river really begins to gain character, passing through its rebellious and energetic teenage stage, if you will. A few miles farther downstream, ancient glaciers have carved out a series of deep gorges in what is now called Wilmington Notch. As it tumbles through these gorges, the river takes on the personality by which it is chiefly known. The rocky West Branch is extremely scenic here, with one of the most dramatic spots being about a mile upstream of the Wilmington Notch State Campground. Here, the river roars over a falls that is more than 100 feet high. Through the millennia, the countless billions of gallons of water churning over this great falls (called High Falls) have gouged out a deep pool within which large trout can hide amid the boulders and ledges. The trout here are comparatively safe both from anglers and from the large chunks of ice that come crashing down each spring when the ice breaks up in the slower sections upriver.

For the next 2 miles, the river sort of catches its breath as it forms numerous pools and pockets before taking another spectacular plunge over another series of falls known today as the Flume. Beneath this falls, there is another large, deep pool that has become famous over the years and where big trout are taken each spring after ice-out. There is rarely a day during the open trout season when there aren't anglers lining the ledges along both sides of this pool. Surprisingly, in spite of the pressure, most of them catch some fish. Over the years, I have taken many good trout in the 15- to 20-inch range and can recall a half dozen or more lunkers that weighed from 4 to 7 pounds. My largest was a 7¼-pound brown taken on a Hornberg streamer.

About a mile below the Flume Falls, the river seems to rest after its arduous journey, and it flows now in a more peaceful fashion until it eventually meets the constraint of a dam located in the center of Wilmington. This is what most of the old-time residents of the village refer to as Lake Everest, but it is merely a dammed up section of stream about 2 miles long, 100 to

400 feet wide, and with depths to about 20 feet. This beat of the West Branch holds some lunkers, and each spring one or two very large trout are bested by lucky anglers fishing the local beach. Recently, for example, an 8½-pounder was taken by one of the local residents. This 2-mile section of slow water above the dam is an ideal spot for bait fishermen, but aside from the section between the bridge in town and the dam, and the small beach section, it must be fished from a small boat.

Beneath this dam at Wilmington, another large pool measuring some 400 feet across holds a great many trout, with some weighing more than 3 pounds. A fairly adept fly fisherman can wade out near the center of the stream below the pool and cast up toward the dam. It is an ideal place to fish large streamers and weighted nymphs. It's also a good spot to try big dry flies just before dark, and in the spring after ice-out, it is one of the favorite pools of bait fishermen.

The section from the Wilmington dam downstream about 2 miles is my favorite stretch for fly-fishing. Here there are pools too numerous to count and pockets formed by converging currents around boulders, and these create excellent fly-fishing water. Access here is difficult, however.

After the river crosses beneath Lewis Bridge below Wilmington, no fishing is allowed for about 1½ miles. Fortunately, this is not one of the better parts of the West Branch. The river here is fairly wide and shallow for the most part, with only a few good holding pools. But from where Black Brook empties into the river at the lower end of the posted water, the river again has an increased number of pools and pockets, and these persist for the next 6 or 7 miles. This beat of river from Black Brook to Ausable Forks is known as "the Bush Country." There are numerous old logging roads from which one can reach the river, but for the most part it has to be gotten to by foot. New subdivisions and posting have made access here more and more difficult. As with the dammed-up section at Wilmington, the ½-mile impounded part of the West Branch above the dam at Ausable Forks contains many trophy-sized fish.

For about a mile below this dam at Ausable Forks, the West Branch offers up some excellent pocket water for the fly fisherman. It is, however, one of the roughest sections of the river to wade. Its bottom is littered with segments of old bridges, broken boulders, and pieces of cement blasted out when the old pulp mills were destroyed years ago.

Now let's get a little bit more specific about a few of the better sections of the West Branch.

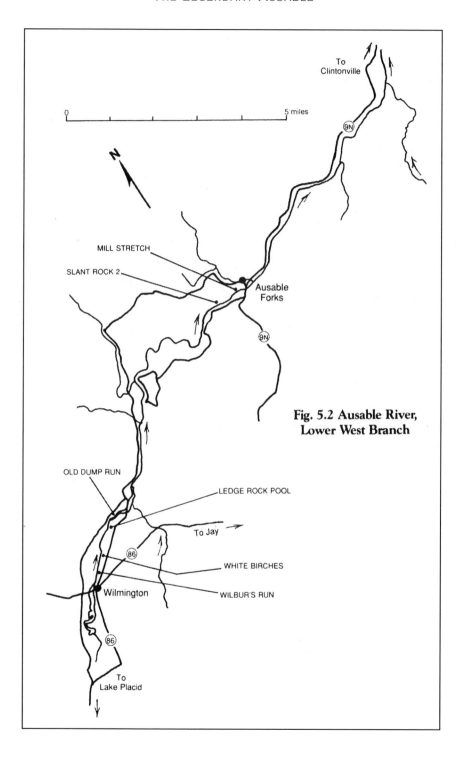

0   5 miles

N

To
Clintonville

9N

MILL STRETCH

SLANT ROCK 2

Ausable
Forks

9N

**Fig. 5.2 Ausable River,
Lower West Branch**

OLD DUMP RUN

LEDGE ROCK POOL

To Jay

86

WHITE BIRCHES

Wilmington

WILBUR'S RUN

86

To
Lake Placid

*Fishing guide releases large brown trout caught in the trophy
stretch of the West Branch of the Ausable River.*

The stretch from the Olympic ski jump outside the village of Lake
Placid down to the NY 86 bridge is, for the most part, deep water with undercut banks, some faster currents, and a few pools. It may be that the largest
trout in the stream are hiding beneath these undercut banks. The Department of Environmental Conservation (DEC) once shocked one of the larger
pools in this section and turned up three trout weighing more than 6 pounds
apiece. (This same scenario also occurs in the mile-long section from the NY
86 bridge down to Monument Falls, where the trophy section begins.) This
section is best fished with nymphs, small streamers, or large wet flies during
the early-season months. At this time, bait fishermen can excel on this part of
the river. During the warmer summer months, small flies in sizes 18 to 22
work best. Terrestrials such as ants and grasshoppers can be a good choice
during the summer period, too. There is also an excellent trico hatch here in
August and September.

From the beginning of the trophy section (discussed below) at Monument Falls all the way down to the Flume, the river is broken water with
plenty of pockets and pools. Much of this is wadable fly-fishing water, and it
is very good. Another of my favorite stretches is the approximately 1-mile

section below the Flume. Here there are a number of islands below which large pools have been formed. These pools produce good-sized trout each spring and fall. This particular section is about 200 feet off NY 86, just north of the Flume bridge.

The West Branch also has some larger tributaries that offer excellent fishing. Black Brook, which empties into the river just below the village of Wilmington, is large enough to fly-fish and produces a good population of fish. I've taken trout weighing up to 4 pounds from this brook. Other West Branch tributaries worth mentioning are Beaver Brook (excellent speckled trout fishing), Little Black Brook, Brown Brook, and White Brook. All of these tributaries are a mile or less from the village of Wilmington.

Seasons and Tips

Many wonder what the best fishing periods are for the various types of fishing possible on the West Branch. From April 1, when the general season opens, until about the middle of May is when bait fishermen often do best. The best natural baits are, of course, minnows and worms. In the faster sections of the West Branch, spinners are often the most effective spinning lures. Included here would be Panther Martins, Mepps, Roostertails, C.P., Swings, or Swiss Swings, etcetera. In the medium to slower sections, Phoebes and Rapalas are often deadly, but they do not operate as well as spinners in the whitewater. During this same period, fly fishermen will do best using small streamers and nymphs fished deep, because the trout are not as active in the cold water and will be close to the bottom. Good early-season patterns are the Grey Ghost, Muddler Minnow, Woolly Worm, and Hornberg.

The best fly-fishing months for the dry-fly fisherman are May, June, July, and September into the middle of October. The first major hatch to emerge is the hendrickson, between the 5th and 10th of May. It is well to remember that the mayfly hatches on the Ausable come off about two weeks later than they do on Catskill streams because of the higher elevation and the colder water temperatures. There are heavy hatches of caddis during May and June and good hatches of stone flies throughout the season. The longest hatch of the year is the *Isonychia bicolor*, which comes off beginning around the middle of August and lasts well into October.

Because much of the river is made up of fast water with many boulders and heavy currents, the most productive flies are usually the larger ones (sizes 10, 12, and 14); smaller flies are often the ticket in the slicks and the pools.

Angler fishes in trophy stretch of West Branch of the Ausable.

The fly that seems to account for more fish than any other is my own Ausable Wulff in sizes 10 and 12. Some of the other especially productive patterns are the dark and light Haystacks, light and dark caddis, Light Cahill, Adams, March Brown, and Hendrickson. The most productive nymph patterns are the black, brown, and light stone fly nymphs, gray mayfly, all-purpose light, Light Cahill, Hendrickson, and blue dun. During July and August, small midges and terrestrials are in order. A good imitation for the *Isonychia* dun is the Dark Haystack with a reddish-brown body.

Another aspect of fishing on the West Branch worth mentioning is the ratio of stocked fish to those spawned in the stream. In the center section of the stream, between Wilmington and the Olympic ski jumps, the trout are mostly stocked fish. A very high percentage of these fish are brown and rainbow trout. From the Olympic ski jump upstream, there is a greater percentage of wild speckled trout (in smaller sizes). From the dam in Wilmington downstream, you will also find a greater percentage of naturally spawned trout, mostly browns and rainbows, but a fair number of speckled trout as well. This 6- or 7-mile section from the dam downstream is the most productive water on the river. Here is where you will find the best fly hatches from May through September.

A word of special advice is in order in regard to wading the West Branch of the Ausable. The river has one of the slipperiest bottoms I have ever encountered, thanks to the algae that covers the rocks, in many areas of the stream. Combine this with the large and often jagged rocks, and you can see why the West Branch is such a treacherous river to wade. It is wise to use both a wading staff and felt-soled waders or felt-soled wading shoes.

Regulations

For the most part, the West Branch is governed by general statewide trout regulations—five trout per day, no size limit, with the season running from April 1 to October 15, except on the "no kill–catch-and-release" section from Riverside Drive through Wilmington Notch, where there is no closed season. This is usually called the trophy section, and here the state stocks large 15-inch brown trout. During the regular trout season, there is probably at least one large trout taken each week from the trophy section.

Since the trophy section was initiated many years ago, it has become a very popular part of the river, for both the novice angler and for those wishing to catch trout without so much of a challenge. Although this section is at times overfished, it produces some excellent opportunities to test your skills at hooking and landing some good-sized trout. Perhaps the best benefit from this 5-mile section is that it reduces pressure on the better sections of the river below the dam at Wilmington.

Be aware that this section of catch-and-release is not limited to fly-fishing only. It's a good place to take novice spin fishermen as well. It's recommended that those fishing with spinning rods use a single-hook lure to make it easier to release the fish. Small spinner flies work exceptionally well. Remember that bait is prohibited in this section.

The Main Stem

Just downstream of the bridge in the center of Au Sable Forks, the West Branch converges with its sister stream, the East Branch, to form the main Ausable. Although the main branch contains some trout, it is not considered top-quality trout water. The river is quite wide and shallow for the most part, and it contains a large number of chubs and shiners. A few good pools can be found farther downstream, but as the river is quite shallow, it heats up during the hot summer months and doesn't produce well. Nonetheless, the Main Stem of the Ausable has its devotees, and there are trout to be caught.

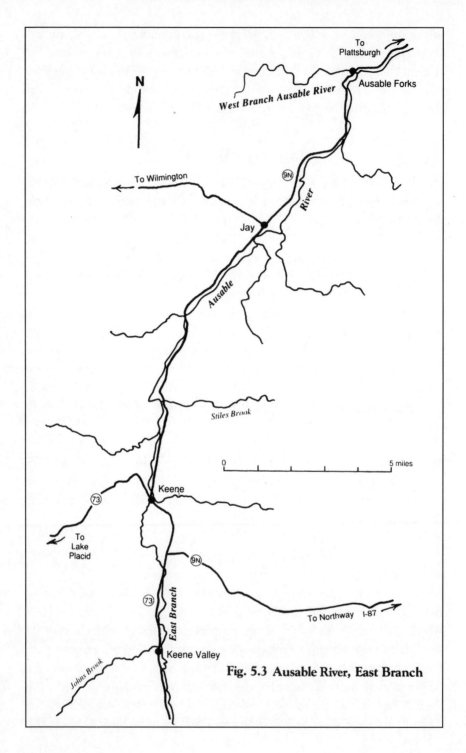

N

To Plattsburgh

West Branch Ausable River

Ausable Forks

To Wilmington

9N

River

Jay

Ausable

Stiles Brook

0   5 miles

Keene

73

To
Lake
Placid

9N

73

East Branch

To Northway   I-87

Johns Brook

Keene Valley

Fig. 5.3 Ausable River, East Branch

The East Branch

The East Branch of the Ausable has its origins in the Ausable Lakes area, southwest of the village of Keene Valley. It flows northward along NY 9N past the villages of Keene, Jay, and Upper Jay. It is a good trout stream by most standards, but it pales alongside the West Branch in terms of both numbers and size of the trout. The East Branch is relatively shallow, without much character, and during the hot months of July and August does not produce well. It is, though, a much tamer river than the West Branch and therefore much easier to wade. There are some good holding pools, and the stream is a good choice for the less-adventurous and less-aggressive angler.

The deeper holding pools and runs are few and far between, so you will have to explore a greater section of the stream to find them. One nice stretch is from Keene upstream to Hull's Falls. Unlike the West Branch, the East Branch has few good feeder streams. Styles Brook and Clifford Brook are the only two tributaries big enough to contain fair populations of fish.

Accommodations

Those visiting this region for the first time will find several types of accommodations. In Wilmington, there are a number of reasonably priced motels.

Many out-of-town anglers who come to fish the Ausable choose a campground as an economical way to spend a few nights. There are a number of choices. One is the Wilmington Notch State Campground, which is located right in the middle of the fishiest section of the river. Another is Adirondack Loj, which offers both indoor lodging and "primitive" outdoor camping. This is located just outside Lake Placid near the South Meadows area and is administered by the Adirondack Mountain Club (ADK). Private campgrounds are also numerous in the Adirondacks and can be found in the various campground directories or through chambers of commerce.

The West Branch of the Ausable is a river worth traveling to, and indeed, some anglers travel thousands of miles to fish its productive waters. It offers all types of fishing conditions for anglers of all dispositions, from the timid to the most adventurous. In fact, many well-known anglers have fished these same waters over the years. Bergman's Run, just upstream of the Flume Pool, is named after Ray Bergman, who did much of his research for his book *Trout* on the Ausable. He often fished this section of stream with my father, and I learned much of my fly-tying technique from this quiet and humble man. "Frustration Pool," located above the trophy section, was named by another good friend and fellow angler, Jim Deren. Jim never missed fishing his favorite pool on his yearly pilgrimages to the Ausable. He fished this pool for the last time only a few months before he passed away.

About the Author

Francis Betters was a fly-tying legend on the West Branch of the Ausable River and a member of the prestigious Catskill Fly Fishing Hall of Fame. He created several now-famous fly patterns, including the Ausable Wulff, Usual, and Haystack. Fran wrote 11 books on fishing and numerous magazine and newspaper articles. He passed away in October 2009 after a long illness.

CHAPTER SIX

In the Heart of the Adirondacks

Brian McDonnell

UPDATED BY DENNIS APRILL

D eep, clear, and cold, Lake Placid lies in the heart of the mountains, at the eastern end of a chain of lakes extending west through the famous Saranac Lakes to scenic Tupper Lake. This so-called Tri-Lakes region of Essex and Franklin counties is a four-season angler's paradise. The large lakes covered in this chapter, together with numerous small ponds, rivers, and brooks in the area, present excellent opportunities for anglers of every taste. Fly-fishing purists will be challenged by the landlocked salmon and trout populations, while worm anglers will enjoy the numerous species of panfish readily caught from boats, bridges, and shorelines.

Lake Placid

Located just outside the 1980 Winter Olympics host village, Lake Placid lies below Whiteface Mountain, the sixth highest of New York's high peaks. This spring-fed, glacial lake, with a gravel- and boulder-strewn bottom and little vegetation, has an average depth of between 60 and 100 feet around its three

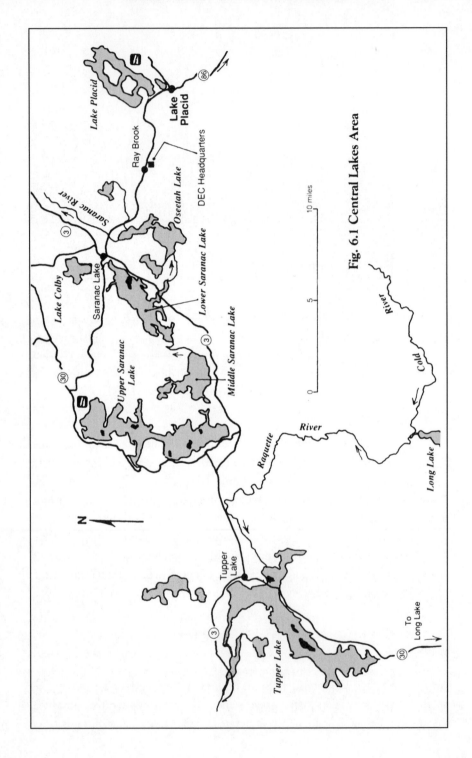

Fig. 6.1 Central Lakes Area

Beaver ponds are commonplace in the heart of the Adirondacks

prominent islands. It is ideal habitat for lake trout, brook trout (speckled trout), and rainbow trout, all of which are found here. There is also a healthy population of smallmouth bass.

Lake trout are best fished early in the spring at ice-out and again in the fall. Slow trolling with spoons or spinners set well back on a flat line is best for surface fishing. A large Lake Clear Wabbler followed by about 16 inches of line, the hook, and a worm, or a Hornburg fly or a streamer, also work well for lakers and brook trout. Fifteen pounds or better is considered trophy-sized lake trout, and 25- to 30-pounders have been taken. The official state record lake trout was caught here in late spring of 1986. That lunker weighed 36 pounds, 8 ounces and was caught on a large spoon trolled slow.

Speckled trout are best fished after ice-out on light tackle when the water is still frigid. Small flies or fly-spinner combinations and other spinners or spoons produce results, as well as a trolled Lake Clear Wabbler or Williams Wabler. A lake map showing deep drop-offs is helpful when fishing for lakers. Rainbow trout are plentiful in Lake Placid, with many 5-plus-pound trophies available. While all of the trout species present reproduce naturally in the lake or its tributaries, New York State's Department of Environmental Conservation (DEC) annually supplements the wild rainbow population with an aggressive stocking program. Rainbow trout are best fished when the lake's surface water warms to more than 60 degrees Fahrenheit.

Lake Placid also supports a healthy smallmouth bass population. They are most common over rocky shoals, uprooted 100-foot white pines along shore, and man-made structures. Artificials, especially old-style wooden plugs and spinnerbaits, work well. Three-pound smallmouths are not un-common. Trophy bass weighing as much as 6 pounds can also be found by the lucky and the skillful. Several large northern pike have come from the lake, including one 18-pounder caught a few years ago. Whitefish, too, are taken on occasion; they are native to Lake Placid but have been on the de-cline the last several decades. Sportspeople are encouraged to return whitefish to the lake unharmed.

There are two excellent public boat launches with facilities, one off Mirror Lake Drive. In the village, lodging, meals, boat rentals, and bait are available.

Because of the slow growth cycle of fish in the northern zone, anglers are encouraged to practice catch-and-release.

Tupper Lake

Best known for its bass and pike fishing, Tupper Lake also offers quality lake trout and landlocked salmon fishing. The village of Tupper Lake has a long history of involvement in the wood products industry, and the lake itself was dammed and enlarged to assist the transport of logs to the mill. The dams created numerous acres of shallow, weedy water and merged Raquette Pond with the main body of Tupper Lake. The expansive, shallow weed beds pro-vide excellent habitat for northern pike, walleye, and bass. Live bait is cus-tomarily used, though white and chartreuse spinnerbait have grown in popularity in recent years.

The main body of the original lake stretches from Watch Island to the South Bay, where the Bog River (or Round Pond Outlet) empties into the lake in grand fashion over Bog River Falls. The numerous rocky islands and weedy shallow bays offer the bass angler a variety of fishing locations. Con-sistent, healthy catches have increased the popularity of the lake among both locals and visiting anglers.

Though Tupper Lake is best known for its warm-water species, anglers, taken with the scenery and pristine beauty of the lake, have discovered a well-kept "local secret"—lake trout and landlocked salmon. The deeper water between Norway Island and Black Point offers a challenging alternative to the normal Tupper Lake regimen. A word of caution: Your day of fishing is best planned for early morning or late afternoon as the prevailing winds blow up the lake on most days.

There is a state-maintained boat launch on NY 30 south of Tupper Lake village. Lodging, restaurants, boat rentals, and live bait are available in the village and around the lake.

Contact the Tupper Lake Chamber of Commerce at 518-359-3328 for more local fishing information and a list of motels and bait and tackle shops.

Lower Saranac Lake and Connected Waters

Located just west of the village of Saranac Lake, the Saranac River connects Lower Saranac Lake to Middle Saranac Lake in the southwest and to Oseetah Lake, Kiwassa Lake, and Lake Flower in the east. The state maintains two sets of locks to allow boat travel among these picturesque bodies of water. Anglers can find tackle shops, live bait, groceries, and a wide variety of restaurants and accommodations for all tastes and budgets. Contact the Saranac Lake Area Chamber of Commerce at 518-891-1990 for more information. Campers can choose from among several area campgrounds or decide to take up residence on one of the many island campsites maintained by the DEC in Lower Saranac Lake. You will need a boat. Rentals are available at several locations around the lakes.

Access to the middle and lower lakes and the chain going into Saranac Lake village can be made through the state-maintained boat ramps on either Lake Flower in Saranac Lake or at First Pond, by the state bridge 3 miles west of Saranac Lake on NY 3. There are several large private boat ramps, and the state maintains canoe and small boat launches at Ampersand Bay on Lower Saranac Lake and on NY 3 at South Creek leading into Middle Saranac Lake. Lower and Middle Saranac lakes were the sites of the 2000–2003 ESPN Great Outdoors Games bass competition.

The predominant sportfishing species in the chain of lakes leading from Lake Flower to Middle Saranac Lake are bass and northern pike. The numerous islands, expansive weed beds, and shallow, stumpy former farmlands

Canoes are useful for fishing the Saranacs

created by the dam on Lake Flower provide excellent habitat and great fishing. Bass in the 1- to 3-pound range are common, while the occasional 5-plus-pound fish has been known to take a popping plug, golden shiner, spinnerbait, purple worm, or crayfish. Northern pike are vicious predators, thus a heavier weight line and a steel leader are recommended for best results. Pike are very opportunistic and often prey on wounded fish, so live bait or a lure resembling a perch or sucker are most effective. Northerns in the 3- to 5-pound range are common, while a 10-plus-pounder will give you all the fight you can handle.

There are numerous good fishing spots on each of the lakes. Concentrate on bass around the islands, rocky shoreline, and prominent structures like felled trees or docks in the early morning and evening. Locally known hot spots on Lower Saranac Lake include Ampersand Bay, Crescent Bay, and the Narrows. Pike can be found in the shallow, weedy bays almost anytime. Best bets are early mornings near the mouth of the Saranac River at the far end of the lake or evenings at the mouth of Fish Creek.

Lake Flower, near the village, is a popular fishing spot for both village residents and summer visitors. Bass and panfish are the primary catches. Oseetah Lake is shallow, stumpy, and loaded with weed beds. Northern pike are plentiful. You may have an opportunity to enjoy competing with an osprey, as they have been known to skim the surface, hook trophy-sized fish in their talons, and return to the top of an old dead pine for dinner.

Kiwassa Lake is tucked away up a channel east of Oseetah Lake. Good-sized pike are caught as they move up the waterway on their way to feed in the lake. The spring bass fishing here, using popping plugs, is excellent.

Lower Saranac is best known for bass, while the angler interested in northern pike will head for Middle Saranac (or Round Lake, as it is known locally). Here, anglers use spinnerbaits around the islands and tease the northerns out of the shallows of the western shoreline by trolling plugs behind a steel leader. A special place for lunch and good fishing, hidden up a navigable waterway off the northern bay of Middle Saranac Lake, is Weller Pond. In all the lakes, the best fishing is in the spring and fall, but quality catches are at times enjoyed even on the hottest days of the summer. At one time, the DEC tried stocking walleye in this lake.

Not to be overlooked in the Tri-Lakes area is ice fishing. The ice fisherman can enjoy some truly fine hard-water fishing in the area. One spot is in Lower Saranac Lake, where an angler can fill his bucket with the large numbers of smelt and yellow perch that winter in the shallow coves and weed beds of the lower lake.

Lake Colby and Upper Saranac

Near Lower Saranac Lake, on NY 86, Lake Colby is another fine example of a year-round angler's paradise. In winter a virtual shantytown appears as ice fishermen establish themselves over their favorite holes. Species sought include rainbow and brown trout, as well as salmon, smelt, splake, and perch. The unofficial close of the ice-fishing season is the annual ice-fishing derby sponsored by the Saranac Lake Fish and Game Club and held the first weekend of March. There are numerous cash and merchandise awards for winners in several categories.

When the ice goes out on Lake Colby, the fish shanties may disappear, but the anglers do not. Canoe and small-boat access is available at the DEC-maintained boat launch on NY 86 across from the General Hospital of Saranac Lake. Brown trout and splake are caught by patient springtime anglers trolling the length of the lake, from the beach to the state boat launch

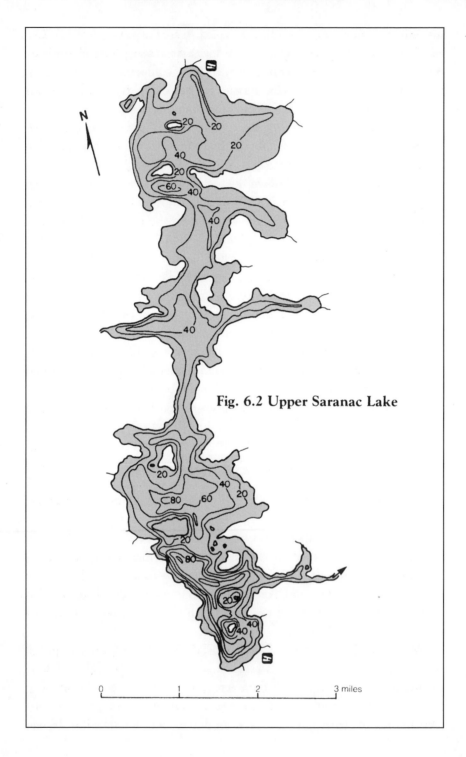

Fig. 6.2 Upper Saranac Lake

site and up the shore in front of DEC's Camp Colby Environmental Education Camp. Rainbows are sought by summertime anglers trolling slowly around the middle of the lake, especially off the point past the former Camp Intermission. Bass fishermen have also discovered the shallows of the western bays of this year-round fishing hole.

Upper Saranac Lake is the largest in the chain, stretching 7 miles from the state-maintained boat ramp at the site of the historic Saranac Inn to the small boat launching site at the end of Indian Carry off NY 3. Some of the deepest water in the Adirondacks, 80 to 100 feet, is found in the area between Chapel Island and the Wawbeek Resort at the southern end of the lake. This deep water annually attracts lake trout fishermen to the upper lake, who anticipate the time when the lakers will be rolling on the water's surface and the chances will be best for landing a trophy fish. A second cold-water game fish, the landlocked salmon, has also become popular among upper lake fishermen. Early-June fly-rod trolling with lead core lines and large streamers is effective. As the summer weather forces the fish deeper, downriggers are useful in getting the lure to the fish.

The rocky, shallow coves and several large islands of Upper Saranac Lake offer anglers a complete change of tackle from that normally used for lakers or salmon. Smallmouth and rock bass are popular summertime species, as are northern pike in the shallow bays of the northern end of the lake. Live bait and spinnerbaits work best in Saginaw or Square bay.

Adding to the diversity of the lake is the ice fishing that can be enjoyed for smelt and yellow perch on any of the bays accessible from NY 30 along the western shore of the lake.

Anglers concentrating on the upper lake can find campsites, groceries, and supplies in Lake Clear or at Fish Creek on NY 30. Comfortable accommodations and meals are also available a short walk from the lake.

Another nighttime fishing activity popular with area residents and visiting campers is the pursuit of bullheads, a bottom-dwelling species present in every lake in the Saranac chain. Night crawlers, a bobber, a lamp or a fire, and a few good friends are all you need for a good night of bullheading.

The diverse opportunities for fishing in the Tri-Lakes and surrounding waterways provide the angler with numerous options within a half-hour drive of a motel room, campsite, or summer home. Cold-water species like lake trout, landlocked salmon, browns, rainbows, and splake; cool-water species like bass and northern pike; good-eating panfish like perch, rock bass, and sunfish; plus social fishing for bullheads in the spring and summer and smelt and perch in the winter—all this combines to make the Tri-Lakes Region a four-season angler's paradise.

About the Authors

Brian McDonnell is a New York State–licensed guide who lives in the Saranac Lake area. Dennis Aprill is the editor of *Good Fishing in the Adirondacks*.

CHAPTER SEVEN

Backcountry Fishing Trips

Dennis Aprill

B ack in the 1880s, hiking into a remote Adirondack pond either with or without a guide and guide boat to fish for native brook trout with a cane fly-rod was considered by many anglers to be the ultimate experience. That experience is still possible today. Granted, there may not be many remote ponds that hold 5-pound brookies, but there are still plenty of backcountry streams and small lakes that are stocked and offer excellent fishing. These are spread throughout the Adirondack Park, but be aware that in many of the ponds above 2,000 feet in the western Adirondacks, fish populations have been wiped out by acid precipitation. So the focus of this chapter will be on the Adirondack heartland, and on one trail in particular that cuts through the center of the park—the Northville–Lake Placid (N-P) Trail—providing access to some great fishing.

The N-P Trail is a winding 120-mile thoroughfare made by the Adirondack Mountain Club in 1922. Its original southern terminus was the Sacandaga River bridge in Northville. Today, most hikers start at Benson, 13 miles to the north. Sections of the N-P Trail are perfect for anglers, because the

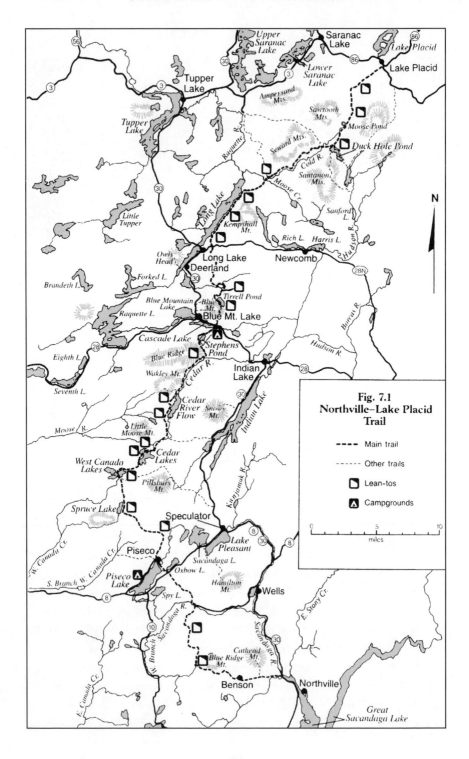

Fig. 7.1
Northville–Lake Placid Trail

- - - Main trail

······ Other trails

☐ Lean-tos

⚠ Campgrounds

Bringing a canoe into the backcountry adds to the fishing opportunities.

winding path follows the valleys and climbs only the passes. It hugs many watersheds that hold trout.

Following is a selection of backcountry fishing opportunities along the N-P. For a detailed description of the trail, call 1-800-395-8080 for a copy of the Adirondack Mountain Club's *Guide to the Northville–Lake Placid Trail.*

Lake Placid–Duck Hole Pond

Duck Hole Pond sits south of Lake Placid, 9.4 miles from the N-P trailhead off Averyville Road. The parking area is on the right, just beyond the Chubb River and the yellow-on-brown Department of Environmental Conservation (DEC) trail marker.

The hike into Duck Hole should be planned as an overnight. There are lean-tos at the pond, but they are often filled, so plan on bringing along a lightweight tent in addition to a sleeping bag, cooking kit, and other camping gear. A four-section spinning or fly-rod packs well. Also bring along an assortment of flies, such as Mickey Finns, Hornbergs, Woolly Buggers, Royal Wulffs, or Adams in sizes 8 to 12. For spinning rigs, smaller spoons such as Little Cleos, Panther Martins, or spinners like those made by Mepps work well.

Sections of the trail into Duck Hole parallel the Chubb River, a narrow stream lined with large tamaracks. The Chubb is stocked with brown trout

Rafting for White-Water Trout

By the time we floated through the second series of haystacks, I finally began to ease up on the rope tied securely to the raft's outer shell. We were rapidly approaching the juncture where the Indian River joins up with the Hudson River. The main thrust of "the bubble," that initial gust from the water release at Lake Abanakee, had passed us by, so we could now float toward our intended campsite at Blue Ledges. The "we" referred to here were three fishermen from the New York City area, myself, and Wayne Failing, our guide. It was late September 1991.

Failing, owner of Middle Earth Expeditions out of Lake Placid, has run rafting trips for more than 25 years and is probably the most seasoned white-water guide on the upper Hudson. This was reassuring, because when he first invited me along, my initial response was: "What class are the rapids?"

"They'll be about class III, with waves only 4 feet high," Failing replied. Having never been white-water rafting, I envisioned an experience akin to riding the Steamin' Demon roller coaster at Great Escape near Glens Falls. This was not the case.

In fact, from the confluence with the Hudson, we began casting into the eddies and holes along the cedar ledges for rainbows and browns. We used the usual assortment of spinning baits, like Mepps, Abu Reflexes, Rooster Tails,

A rafter fishes in the Hudson River near Blue Ledges in Hudson Gorge.
This stretch of the river holds some sizeable brown and rainbow trout.

Splake caught in an Adirondack mountain pond.

and Panther Martins of various sizes. Unfortunately, the rainbows weren't biting, so we focused on the browns, catching and releasing some nice-sized fish.

We were the last ones out of the launch site below Lake Abanakee, so thankfully, we were left to float behind the throng of rafts that congregates on the river on weekends throughout the spring, summer, and fall.

By early afternoon, we had arrived at Blue Ledges, and while Failing set up camp, we fished the rocky shoreline. Luckily, that last weekend in September was a cool one, and most of the campsites at Blue Ledges were empty; as a result, there was little fishing pressure. I took out my old favorite for brown trout, a 4-inch silver Rapala, and worked the slower stretches. Two of the other fellows fanned out downstream, and one who had never caught a freshwater fish before cast in a pool in front of our campsite. As luck would have it, he caught the largest fish of the trip—a 16-inch brown trout weighing 2 pounds.

The next day, Sunday, after fishing the early-morning hours, we once again caught "the bubble" down the Hudson. As we slithered through the Osprey Nest Rapids, Given's Rift, and the Black Hole, we were treated to 360s around rocks, and when there was a shore audience, a few "shake and bake" moves through drop-offs.

From where the Hudson flows under the Delaware and Hudson railroad bridge to North River, trip's end, there are ample fishing opportunities, especially where the Boreas River joins the Hudson.

Failing runs rafting/fishing trips throughout the spring and fall when the town of Indian Lake allows water releases from Abanakee Dam. In the spring, I am told, with class V rapids, things can get a little hairy. Middle Earth Expeditions can be reached at 518-523-9572 or online at www.adirondack rafting.com.

This hiker fishes a remote Adirondack pond for brook trout.
Solitude and a chance to catch wild native brook trout are reasons why
many like to backpack in with their fishing gear.

and also holds some brook trout. Pause along the way to do some fishing. The water just below Wanika Falls, some 4 miles from the trailhead, is especially worth a stop.

Duck Hole is stocked by air with 2,800 brook trout each spring. Besides the usual spinning lures and dry flies, worms are great fish producers here. You won't need a fancy rig, just some small split shot, or better yet, let the worm sink naturally without added weight.

Day Trip South of Lake Durant

From the trailhead at the Lake Durant Campground off NY 28/30, 3 miles east of Blue Mountain Lake, the N-P goes south, reaching Stephens Pond at 2½ miles. Stephens is stocked annually with 1,300 brown trout and can easily be fished from the shoreline.

One mile west of Stephens is Cascade Pond, a small pond that is stocked by air with 2,400 brook trout. Cascade can be reached by a marked side trail that heads northwest of Stephens Pond.

From Cascade Pond, the trail goes west, then north to Lake Durant (a cool-water fishery stocked with tiger muskellunge) and NY 28/30. The 1-mile walk back to the parking area at the campground is on hardtop highway. Alternatively, you can leave another vehicle at the roadside near the cemetery off NY 28/30, ¾ of a mile east of Blue Mountain Lake Village.

Piseco North

The N-P Trail north of Piseco Lake is the gateway to the remote West Canada Lake Wilderness and some of the best brook trout fishing in the Adirondacks. From Piseco village, the N-P goes north for 3 miles, then veers northwest, crossing the Jessop River after 7½ miles and arriving at Spruce Lake in 10 miles. Spruce is stocked by air with over 5,000 brook trout. there are three lean-tos at this lake for overnight camping.

From Spruce, the N-P continues north 6 miles into the heart of the wilderness area and to three major brook-trout-stocked lakes: West Canada Lake, South Lake, and Mud Lake. West Canada Creek, the outlet, is also an excellent brook trout water, but some bushwhacking is required to reach the brook's headwaters.

Each of the three lakes has a lean-to nearby (West Canada has two), but be prepared to camp out, as this area is popular during July and August, probably the slowest months for brook trout fishing. For serious anglers, early May and late September are the best times to fish for brookies. During these times, you'll also find fewer people and almost no blackflies, the scourge of the Adirondacks in late May and early June.

Trip Pointers

For overnights, try to keep your pack weight in the 30-pound range. Bring along a tent in case lean-tos are full, but remember that no camping is allowed within 150 feet of water. Be sure to follow the number-one rule of camping etiquette: carry out what you bring in. Stow food safely with cable or rope suspended from a tree limb so as not to attract bears. Finally, practice catch-and-release, or keep only the fish you intend to eat that day.

About the Author

Dennis Aprill is the editor of *Good Fishing in the Adirondacks*.

Ice fishing is a popular winter activity on Schroon Lake.

CHAPTER EIGHT

The Peaceful Schroon Lake Area

Val De Cesare Sr.

UPDATED BY VAL DE CESARE JR.

C radled at the foot of Pharaoh Mountain is a 9-mile lake that offers visitors a panoramic view of the Adirondack Mountains. Schroon Lake begins at a point some 5 miles north of Chestertown and extends to 1 mile north of Schroon Lake village. Schroon is a very pretty lake with deep blue waters. It has a surface area of 4,230 acres and maximum depth of 152 feet. Although it is about 9 miles long, the lake's widest point, off Adirondack village at the southern end, is only about 1½ miles. The lake's north–south axis parallels US 9 between exits 26 and 28 of the Northway. Northbound motorists should get off at exit 26 from I-87 and head north on US 9; those heading southbound should use exit 28 and head south on US 9.

There are two public boat launches on Schroon Lake. One is in the village of Schroon Lake and is free. The other, in the town of Horicon at the southern tip of Schroon Lake, is a state-owned boat launch and is also free. There is a marina at the northern tip of the lake that will accommodate all of your boating needs. You may also moor your boat there between fishing

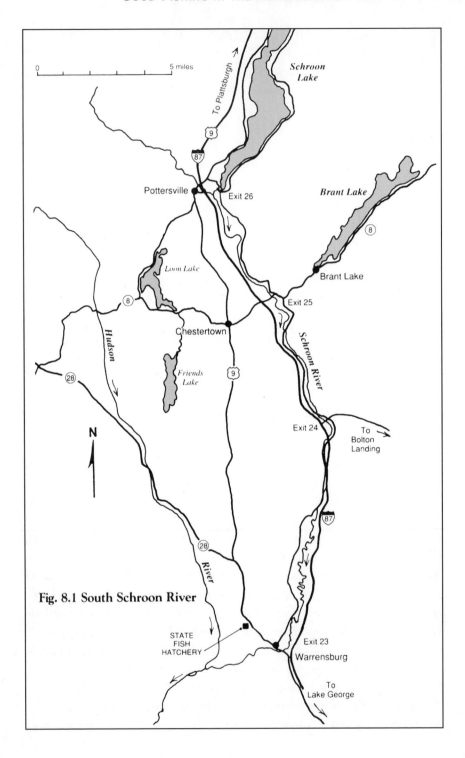

Fig. 8.1 South Schroon River

trips. Year-round fishing is permitted for most species, though northern pike is closed between March 15 and May 1.

Fishing Tips

Schroon Lake contains a wide array of sport fish, including salmon, lake trout, and smallmouth and largemouth bass. Schroon Lake also supports a healthy panfish population with yellow perch, sunfish, and crappie. Last but not least by any means is the prized northern pike, with 16- to 20-pounders caught annually.

Spring fishing tends to be the most exciting around ice-out. Landlocked salmon and lake trout are excited with the onset of the smelt spawning run. Stickbaits and spoons imitating a smelt or small perch will surely trigger a hookup when trolled in the 2- to 3-mile-per-hour range. Concentrate on the river to the north and small streams around the lake, especially the Millbrook, which is located right in town. Feeding fish will usually rise at sunup and sundown, which will help you locate them. Don't forget the river itself.

Rapalas, ThunderSticks, and other stickbaits are my favorites. Needlefish, Mooselooks, and small spoons also hold their own. Stick with "natural" colors such as silver, gold, and rainbow trout for your lure selection. Troll them slowly in cold, 38- to 40-degree water, faster when the water warms. Keep your speed to the 2- to 4-mile-per-hour range.

Trolling with streamer flies can also be exciting when action heats up. Try a Sebago Smelt or a Grey Ghost or any slim minnow pattern with green or purple. Flies should be trolled 2½ to 5 miles per hour and twitched or jerked quite often. Concentrate on the shallows where lures won't run, especially the north end river basin. Nothing beats a 4-pound landlocked salmon on a 7-foot rod.

Fishing in the summer for lake trout and salmon can be a little more difficult. Downriggers, drop weights, and lead core line will help you get to the thermocline. This is where salmon and lake trout reside in the summer. You will also find a healthy population of lake trout on the bottom. Troll downriggers in the 25- to 40-foot range for salmon and lake trout. Use the same stickbaits and spoons you used in the spring. Don't be afraid to use some orange or chartreuse this time of year. Green and silver prism needlefish work well when trolled about 2½ to 3 miles per hour.

Trolling the bottom can be very exciting for lake trout in the summer. Handlining with copper using large spoons in deeper pockets around 70 to

80 feet will also rouse sleeping lunkers. Troll very slowly on the bottom. Steel or braided line with a 3- to 4-ounce drop weight to get to the bottom is very effective. Fish a Lake Clear with a fly or cut bait 12 inches behind a spoon. Troll depths of 55 to 80 feet about 1 to 1½ miles per hour. Big lakers get very lazy in the summer, so don't be afraid to slow way down.

One of the local favorite spots to fish lake trout is the area immediately west of Sola Bella Island, also known as Clark's Island and Word of Life Island. Troll north–south about 200 yards west of the island, principally covering the southern half. Then head from the southern tip of the island west toward Grove Point. Another favorite spot for forktails is the easterly shore of the narrows. This water is approximately 60 to 80 feet deep.

Probably the most productive area for lunker lakers is in the southern half of the lake. There is a sunken island between Adirondack village and Schroon Manor that is always well marked with buoys. Try all around this spot, especially where the water is 50 to 80 feet deep (which is primarily north and west of Sunken Island). There is an 8-foot channel that runs north–south between Schroon Manor and Eagle Point. Fish the shallower portions of this channel early in the year, and then go deeper as the water warms.

Another good lake spot runs from Adirondack village north toward the Narrows. This area is very uneven in depth and not very well defined as to direction. If you want, just try to hold to about a 50-foot depth. Don't worry if your depth varies. Going south from Adirondack village along the east shore, I would hold between 50 and 80 feet.

In the fall, as the surface temperature drops to approximately 55 degrees, salmon and lake trout may again be caught on the surface. Use the same techniques and lures as for spring fishing for these species.

Ice Fishing

Fishing through the ice is probably the most effective way to land lunker lake trout and salmon. Schroon Lake and most of the surrounding ponds freeze up solid by about December 20, give or take 10 days.

Fowler Avenue and Dock Street provide the ice fisherman with two excellent access points to the northern portion of Schroon Lake. Just out from Fowler Avenue on the west shore is a good drop-off for lakers and salmon. Dock Street usually provides good vehicular access to the whole northern basin. Again, the area west of the island is excellent. Another good spot is

As soon as the ice hardens anglers flock to Schroon Lake for ice fishing.

the eastern shore below the island. Shanties are usually very much in evidence over the better locations. The central portion of the lake is probably best in the general vicinity of the Narrows. Access to this area can be made via Hayes Road off US 9, or over the bank by the Narrows Restaurant.

About a mile south of exit 27 (northbound only) off I-87 is Eagle Point Campsite. Just north and south of the campsite along the eastern shoreline is another good area to fish. Access is obtained through the campsite or parking farther south and walking out onto the lake.

Continuing south along US 9 and just north of the town Pottersville, we take a right onto the River Road. Cross the Schroon River bridge and pass the state boat launch at Horicon, then go left on East Shore Road. Approximately 4 miles to the north, you will see the village of Adirondack, where Mill Brook enters Schroon Lake. This is a good access point to fish the east shore of the southern basin. Fish fairly close to shore to the south, and go farther away from shore to the north. Again, there should be some shanties out to guide you.

Live smelt suspended about 10 to 15 feet below the ice seem to produce the most fish, but dead smelt are sometimes just as effective. (Smelt may be purchased at the local bait stores.) I like to stay in waters that are between 30 and 60 feet deep, but I have seen fish caught in waters up to 80 and 100 feet deep. If smelt are unavailable, suckers or shiners may do the trick.

Each angler is allowed five tip-ups and two hand lines. Bait, tackle, and licenses are available in Schroon Lake.

A key to success in most of these Adirondack lakes is light tackle. Small hooks in the 6 to 10 range and 4- to 8-pound-test line will greatly increase your success. Most of my catches have come on minnows fewer than 3 inches long. Always maintain your tip-up holes. Keeping your equipment free from ice will certainly help.

There are many food establishments open in Schroon Lake for winter anglers, but motel accommodations are more limited. And advance reservations are recommended.

Warm-Water Species

While landlocks and lakers provide much action here, there are many other fish present in Schroon Lake. These include smallmouth and largemouth bass, northern pike, yellow perch, smelt, calico bass, rock bass, sunfish, suckers, and various minnows.

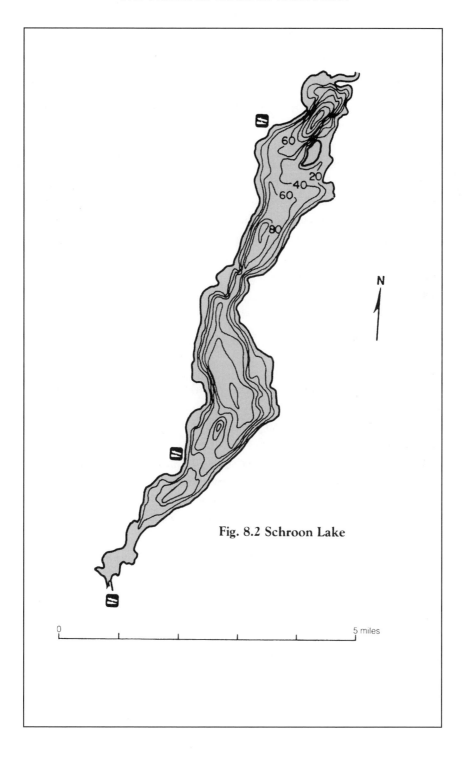

Fig. 8.2 Schroon Lake

Smallmouth bass prefer rocky shelves and shoals. Largemouth bass (not very abundant) prefer the weedy portion of the north basin, in the bay directly opposite Fowler Avenue on the east shore: around a rock pile just north of the public beach in Schroon Lake village and a good mess of rocks running westerly off the southern tip of the island (this bunch of rocks runs about halfway across the lake and then drops off into 80 feet of water); by a big rock shelf off the Narrows Restaurant (this runs from the east shore about halfway across the lake); and around the Sunken Island in the south basin. Remember one thing: the shallower areas around these shoals are excellent habitat for the cool-water species such as bass, perch, pike, and panfish, while the deeper areas are excellent habitat for trout and salmon.

A little-known secret about Schroon Lake is its crappie population. Small pockets of large crappie are found throughout the lake. Lockwood Bay, at the north end of the lake, is a good place to start. Veteran crappie fishermen will have no problem finding prime structure for a few slabs.

Paradox Lake

About 3 miles northeast of Schroon Lake lies Paradox Lake. This lake derives its name from an old Indian word that means "flowing backward." During the spring, when the thaw is at its peak, the Schroon River (and Paradox Creek tributary) actually reverses its flow back into Paradox Lake. For a short time, Paradox Lake has no outlet.

Five-mile-long Paradox Lake has a maximum depth of 52 feet and a surface area of 860 acres. It is divided into two halves, with a narrow, streamlike portion dividing the two sections. The eastern sector has a maximum depth of 27 feet. It is the home of most of the cool-water species of fish that reside in Paradox.

To get to Paradox Lake, take I-87 to exit 28, then go east along NY 74 about 1 mile. There is a public boat launch at the state campsite located about 3 miles farther along NY 74. There is a fee for parking. Most of your supplies should be bought in advance.

Paradox Lake has lake trout, few landlocked salmon, rainbow trout, smallmouth and largemouth bass, great northern pike, pickerel, lake herring, bullhead, perch, calico bass, and numerous other panfish. Rainbow trout and all of the cool-water fish are spread throughout the lake. The lake trout here are concentrated primarily in the western sector. Trolling for lake trout is done much the same as it is in Schroon Lake. Most of the productive waters

Northern pike is only one of several species that make braving the cold worthwhile for an angler and his fishing partner.

are around the rim of the 52-foot depth. The inlet to Paradox Lake lies at its easternmost end. There are mostly weedy beds and shallow shelves near here.

These make for good winter fishing for perch. Winter perch are the best fish for eating.

The outlet of Paradox begins at the westernmost end of the lake and flows (except in spring) until it enters Schroon River just south of NY 74. This is a slow-flowing stream and has been known to produce some good-sized brown trout. Of course, you have to get back off the main road and be there in late spring or early summer.

Paradox Lake has produced lake trout in the 16- to 20-pound class, rainbow trout up to 8 pounds, largemouth bass more than 6 pounds, and northern pike more than 24 pounds. There are some tackle-busters in there yet that will beat these.

The prime lake trout area in Paradox Lake is at the western end of the lake. It resembles a triangle that begins at the western end of the narrow (Brier Point), carrying due west to a point jutting out into the lake from the western end of Grovesnor Bay, then due south to a boathouse, then easterly back to Brier Point. The maximum water depth of this area is 52 feet.

Largemouth bass and northern pike are caught in the weedy sections in the easternmost part of the lake and in the narrows. Fishing through the ice at Smiths Bay (Nawita Bay) has produced some lunker pike. Pike weighing 22 to 24 pounds have been caught there.

Perch can be caught in almost every corner of the lake. Fishing for perch in the winter is a favorite pastime for local anglers. Most of it is done on the eastern end of the lake and in Nawita Bay.

Smallmouth bass can be caught at either end of the lake. Fish for them off the rocky ledges with surface lures cast from about just before and after dark. Any of your favorites should work here. You can troll for rainbow trout at either end of the lake. Most anglers use a set of spinners with a trailing night crawler. Troll the lure about 10 to 15 feet down.

Paradox Lake also contains a healthy crappie population. These can be located in Nawita Bay and at the east end of the narrows. Small fathead minnows and a number 10 hook are your best bet. A slip bobber rig is essential.

The Schroon River

The portion of the Schroon River that flows into Schroon Lake will be the only part of the river discussed here. It begins at a point just south of exit 30 of the Northway and flows south for about 17 miles before entering the lake. These 17 miles would be as the crow flies—the river actually zigzags along for probably 40 miles or more.

Several miles south of exit 30, the river first crosses US 9 from east to west. This is known as Deadwater Bridge. This, for all practical purposes, is the beginning of the northern portion of the Schroon River. About a mile south of Deadwater Bridge, the river crosses US 9 again, this time from west to east. There is a public campsite at this crossing (Sharp's Bridge Campsite). Between Deadwater Bridge and Sharp's Bridge, Landsey Brook enters the Schroon River. Almost exactly ½ mile farther south along US 9, there is a small trail that turns right down a slight hill. This is the road that leads to West Mill Brook. It is a wilderness road, traversable by most, but not all, vehicles. Greenough Road is another access point to the Schroon River. It lies just about 2 miles below the Sharp's Bridge Campsite.

The section between Sharp's Bridge and Greenough Road winds away from any roads for about 2 miles. This is one of the best runs on the Schroon River, and it's a good place to spend a day.

VAL DE CESARE JR.

A nice brown trout taken from the Schroon River.

Just about a mile south of Greenough Road is Pepper Hollow Road. By taking a right on this road, you will first cross West Mill Brook, and then you will meet the Schroon River again. The river parallels the road along its full length. The river is now west of US 9 and will not cross again until Schroon River Falls, which is about 9 miles farther south. Between Pepper Hollow Road and Black Brook Road (the Port Henry Road) is another section of the river that can be very productive for both brook and brown trout. In between there is one other road crossing the Frontier Town in the hamlet of North Hudson. This is where the Branch, a tributary flowing east from the Blue Ridge, also joins the Schroon River.

This entire section of the Schroon watershed is well stocked with brook trout and brown trout. There are trout in all the tributaries as well. The Branch is almost entirely posted by private clubs, and permission to fish it is difficult, but possible, to obtain. Again it should be emphasized that the better fishing would be away from the roads and beaten paths.

The stretch above North Hudson is primarily small-stream fishing. Here it is probably best to fish the old-fashioned way—by wading the stream. A flat-bottom boat or a shallow-running canoe may be used in some sections, but it will be necessary to get out and portage around many obstacles and sandbars. Speckled trout weighing a pound or better have been caught in this section of the Schroon, but be careful in identifying trout. Young salmon are at times very plentiful in this sector. Please be careful in releasing them.

Below North Hudson, the Schroon River becomes larger and lazier. It meanders its way south and has very little fast water. This is a very good section to fly-fish for some sassy brown trout. Fall fly-fishing has also produced some healthy acrobatic salmon in this section. Even lake trout and pike have been caught this far north during the sucker spawning runs in the spring right after ice-out. This section is best handled by floating a small flat-bottom boat or canoe. There are no major obstacles to the falls at US 9.

Spring fishing for salmon and lake trout is very good in late April and early May in the Schroon River just above where it enters the lake. Trolling a Grey Ghost or other smelt imitation or a small floating Rapala works very well. Once you tangle with a 3-pound or larger salmon in the river, you will be hooked for life.

Trout Brook

Trout Brook is a beautiful stream of pure mountain waters. It lies about 6 miles to the west of Schroon Lake, flows from the north to south parallel to the lake, then turns east to join the Schroon River below the lake. Trout Brook begins in the Hoffman Notch Wilderness Area, and then flows south toward Olmsteadville. It is well stocked with speckled trout, and there is a head of naturally bred trout in the upper reaches and tributaries. If you ever had the desire to taste a meal of freshly caught native brook trout, this is the stream to fish. It is posted in many locations, but permission to cross private lands may sometimes be obtained via a polite request. The best fishing opportunities lie in the upper reaches, where the fish are small but wonderfully good to eat.

To get to this brook, take Hoffman Road, which is located just south of Schroon Lake village on US 9. Go west for about 6 miles to what is known as Olmsteadville Road. Just before hitting this road, you will cross a small stream. This is Trout Brook. Topographic maps will show some access spots north of this point. (There aren't any road crossings above here.) Turning south, you will cross the brook in several spots. Going south of the next bridge takes you to an area of slow-moving water and many beaver dams. This is a good section to fish from a canoe or flat-bottom boat.

Other Nearby Adirondack Waters

Probably the most beautiful and bountiful fisheries in the area are the vast number of backwoods ponds. Crane Pond and Goose Pond are easily accessed via Crane Pond Road, off Schroon's East Shore Road and Alder Meadow Road. Goose Pond is about a ¾-mile hike. The pond is well stocked with brookies and splake, as well as other trout species. Crane Pond is accessible with a car, so anglers with limited mobility can give this pond a try. Crane Pond is also stocked with several trout species, as well as cool-water fish species.

The waters and wetlands of the Schroon drainage, like all those in the Adirondack Forest Preserve, are of extraordinary value. They support a wide range of wildlife. They are also a natural recreation area affording unlimited opportunities for bird-watching, wildlife observation, photography, and canoeing, as well as fishing, hunting, and trapping. Please use the utmost care when visiting all these wild areas. Carry out what you carry in and don't bury anything unless it is readily biodegradable. Make sure all fires are out before you leave camp.

The Schroon Lake region is one of the most beautiful in New York State. If visitors use it wisely, it can remain so.

About the Authors

The late Val De Cesare Sr. was an avid fisherman and outdoorsman who lived in the Schroon Lake area. He knew the Schroon watershed and surrounding waters as well as anyone. Val Jr. continues his father's tradition, fishing the Schroon area with his wife, Diane, and his son, also named Val, year-round.

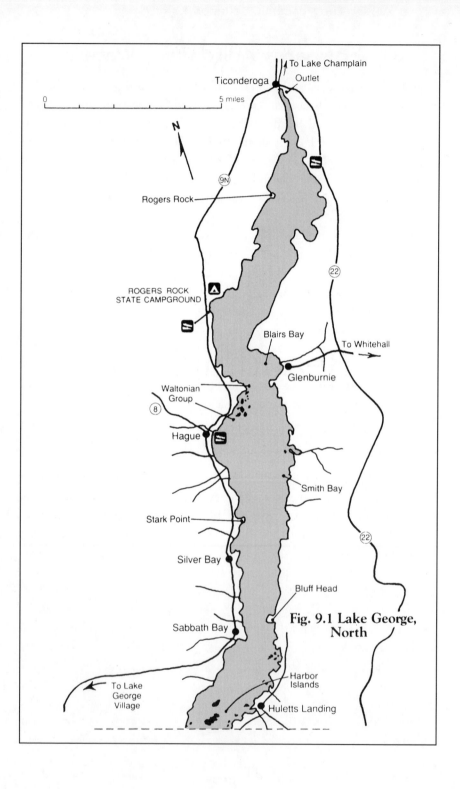

0   5 miles

N

To Lake Champlain
Ticonderoga   Outlet

9N

Rogers Rock

ROGERS ROCK
STATE CAMPGROUND

Blairs Bay   To Whitehall

22

Glenburnie

Waltonian
Group

8

Hague

Smith Bay

Stark Point

22

Silver Bay

Bluff Head

Sabbath Bay

Fig. 9.1 Lake George,
North

To Lake
George
Village

Harbor
Islands

Huletts Landing

CHAPTER NINE

Lake George: America's Most Beautiful Lake

Dan Ladd

I n the summer of 1642, a French Jesuit priest named Father Isaac Jogues became the first white man to witness the picturesque beauty and crystal clear waters of Lake George. Jogues had traveled south from Canada via the Richelieu River and Lake Champlain, whereupon reaching this great body of water named it Lake of the Holy Sacrament (Lac du Saint-Sacrement). As a missionary, his purpose was to convert the Iroquois to Christianity, but his arrival coincided with an epidemic among the tribe. They blamed Father Jogues, who then was subjected to numerous tortures and eventually was beheaded with the blow from a tomahawk. Thus the "Mission of the Martyrs" was sealed with the blood of the lake's European discoverer.

Few lakes in our country can rival either the scenic grandeur or the historical significance of Lake George. Its present name was given by Sir William Johnson, who in the early days of the French and Indian War (1754–1763) led his militia north while the colonies were still under the rule of King George II. In literature, James Fenimore Cooper's legendary fictional characters from *The Last of the Mohicans*—Hawkeye, Chingachgook, and Uncas—came from the Leatherstocking country to fight near Fort William Henry. Fort Ticonderoga on Lake Champlain, located at the foot of Lachute Rapids, was paramount for control for the most important north–south waterway in the colonies. In the latter half of the 18th century, this region was the violent setting for numerous contests as France and England fought for control of the continent, and the colonists for their freedom. Visiting anglers who are also history buffs should expand their itineraries to include visits to Fort Ticonderoga, Fort William Henry, and Crown Point.

Overview

Lake George, sometimes called the Queen of American Lakes, is a product of the late Pleistocene epoch, also known as the great Ice Age. It was formed by the scouring retreat of a great glacier that left natural dams on its north and south ends. Runoff from the Adirondacks to the west and the Green Mountains to the east feed its 32-mile length. Rarely more than a mile and a half wide, with a notable maximum depth of 200 feet, the lake offers over 28,000 acres of premier fishing for a variety of species. It is easily reached from the Adirondack Northway (I-87) as exits 20 through 28 will bring you to the lake and its approximately two hundred islands.

The New York State Department of Environmental Conservation (DEC) maintains 387 shoreline campsites on 44 of those islands for overnight camping by permit only (no dogs). This allows anglers to have rods in the water even while the breakfast bacon is frying. An additional 116 day-use sites on eight islands are maintained and can provide a picturesque setting for a tasty shore lunch.

Lake George is naturally divided into two distinct sections: the north and south basins. While both have deep waters and islands, the north basin is much narrower, and its shores are primarily state forest preserve lands and thus undeveloped. It also is home to most of the islands, including the Narrows and Mother Bunch groups. Like Lake Champlain, Lake George is another two-story fishery of impressive dimension. It offers warm- and cool-water fishing for largemouth bass, smallmouth bass, northern pike, pickerel, and panfish (mainly perch and crappie), as well as good opportunities for its cold-water residents, landlocked salmon and lake trout.

Boat Launches

While Lake George sports a number of marinas along its shores that charge a fee for boat launching, there are a few public boat launches as well. The Lake George Beach State Park in Lake George Village provides access to the south basin but is closed from Memorial Day weekend through Labor Day. Other public boat launches are located in Bolton Landing, Hague, and Ticonderoga. Fee launching can also be found at Rogers Rock Campground. A car-top-only boat launch is located on Northwest Bay Brook.

All vessels 8 feet or longer or any boats powered by a 10-horsepower or greater motor must be registered with the Lake George Park Commission and display a registration decal. Permits are available on an annual basis, by the week or for one day.

Bass Fishing

In most of New York, regular bass season opens the third Saturday in June and closes on November 30. Catch-and-release fishing is now allowed the remainder of the year. Fishing for largemouth and smallmouth bass can be great from late spring and onward through summer and into early autumn. The spawn for both species can vary based on water temperature but usually has completed by mid-June.

Open water after the breakup of ice. Lake George was called America's most beautiful lake by Thomas Jefferson.

DAN LADD

Lake George has a very good largemouth bass fishery.

From opening day of the regular bass season until mid-July, the large-mouths can be found fairly shallow in the many bays, such as Weeds, Blairs, Dark, Gull, and Indian in the North Basin and Huddle, Boon, Harris, and Dunham's in the South Basin as well as the fen in Northwest Bay. During this time of the year, these fish can be caught around docks, around sub-merged wood, and in milfoil and other vegetation in the backs of the bays. Lures of choice in these situations would be ¼- to ½-ounce black and blue jigs with plastic or pork trailers. Another good choice would be a 4- or 6-inch black or red shad plastic worm. Bass fishermen do well with most plas-tics, including Senko worms, Sweet Beavers, and their various imitations.

Top-water baits such as the Zara Spook, Rapalas, or the Pop-R are all excellent choices when you wish to cover a lot of water while looking for active fish. As the water warms in mid-July, the largemouth bass head for deeper waters, such as that in the 20- to 25-foot range. These fish can also be caught on a regular basis, but it takes a totally different technique: Carolina rigging. To Carolina rig, you use a ¾-ounce egg sinker, a plastic bead, a barrel swivel, and a 3-foot leader. The hook is then baited with a plastic lizard or worm. The rig, which is dragged along the bottom of the deep water, is excellent for catching bass. It is also not uncommon for anglers to find bucketmouths in vegetation in aforementioned bays.

The smallmouth bass tend to stay along the rocky areas in the lake, which include Block Point, Coates Point, Hawkeye Point, Anthony's Nose, Friend's Point, and the many sunken islands in the North Basin. The numerous islands found in the narrows can also be excellent places to find smallmouths. In the southern end of the lake, islands such as Dome, Elizabeth, Long, Canoe, Phelps, and Diamond are excellent choices.

Smallmouth bass will stay shallow until around July 1. They can be easily caught using chartreuse spinnerbaits, pumpkinseed-colored jigs with pork combos, and top-water bait such as the Pop-R or Sluggo. As the water warms, smallmouths move into deep water that ranges from 30 to 90 feet. These fish can be caught on jigging spoons such as a ½-ounce Hopkins Shorty, jigging just off the bottom. Carolina rigging may be another alternative. You will also find bronzebacks in Lake George along many of the steep, rocky drop-offs found throughout the lake. Study of a lake contour map will indicate these areas, and use of electronics to find suspended fish is paramount. Drop-shot rigs and deep diving crankbaits are common presentations, as well as working football jigged plastics retrieved at a slow to moderate pace.

There are several bass tournaments held on Lake George every year, including those by the New York State Bass Chapter Federation and the Adirondack Bass Club. Because of the wind, most launches take place at Mossey Point and at the Hague boat launches in the North Basin.

Other Warm-Water Species

The northern pike and pickerel seasons begin the first Saturday in May and close annually on March 15. The best fishing is during the spring when the pike and pickerel are still in shallow water. They can be caught easily using lures (such as orange, chartreuse, or white spinnerbaits, or Rapala-type plugs in a perch or smelt pattern) or live bait (such as shiners or sucker minnows). As the water warms, the fish tend to move deep, just like the bass. Covering a lot of water in the 30- to 40-foot range by trolling plugs or using live bait can be very productive. Good places to look for the pike and pickerel are the weed beds in the areas of Bolton Landing, Warner Bay, or Dunham's Bay. Also, Northwest Bay and Harris Bay in the South Basin and Blair Bay in the North Basin are good bets. The lake has a good population of pike and pickerel, with the pike averaging 4 to 6 pounds and the pickerel averaging 3 to 5 pounds. That said, there are some very large pike in Lake George, and many are pulled through the ice during the winter.

Panfishing in Lake George is productive year-round. Both crappie and yellow perch can be easily caught. In the spring, large crappies can be caught in shallow water off wooden docks along the shorelines in Bolton Landing, Huddle Bay, or Dunham's Bay. Small white and chartreuse hair jigs, tube jigs, or small minnows on a bobber seem to be what attracts the crappies best. The rest of the year, the crappies can be found in 20 to 25 feet of water near wooden structures. The yellow perch in Lake George can be caught just about anywhere in the lake where grass is on the bottom and in 25 to 40 feet of water. Light blue line baited with small jigging spoons, small hair jigs, rubber jigs, or live bait has proven to be very productive when fishing for yellow perch. The average-sized perch weighs about 1 pound; a large one is in the 2-pound range.

Perch are another popular ice fishing species.

Trout and Salmon

Lake George's cold-water species are its most popular as the lake has blossomed into a major lake trout fishery. Lakers can be fished year-round with a minimum creel length of 23 inches and a daily limit of two. Lake trout are no longer stocked in Lake George as they reproduce naturally. The salmon fishing is not what it once was, but landlocked Atlantic salmon remain a heavily stocked and often targeted species. Salmon can also be fished year-round with a minimum length of 18 inches and a daily limit of two. The use and/or possession of rainbow smelt for bait or consumption is prohibited on Lake George. Smelt remain the primary forage for both lake trout and salmon.

In the spring, when the smelt are spawning in the many creeks that empty into the lake, the trout and salmon can be found in the shallow waters feeding on these fish. Trolling the shorelines with planer boards rigged with trolling spoons, small Rapalas, or other stickbaits seem to work well.

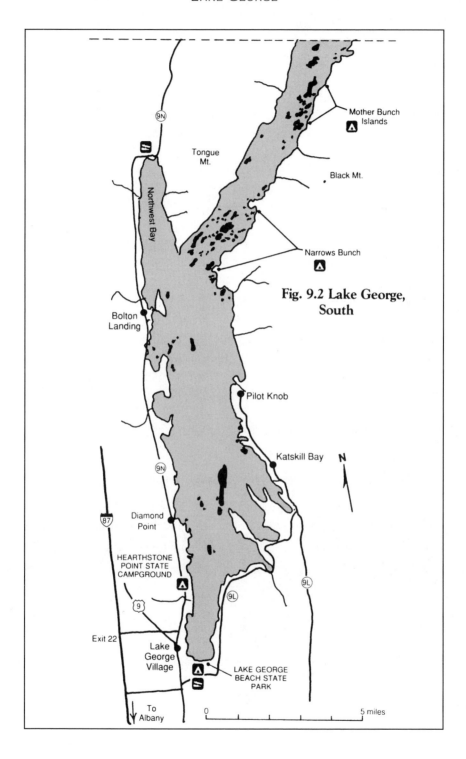

Fig. 9.2 Lake George, South

Spoons such as Evil Eyes, Suttons, Mooselook Wobblers, and Heddons, and stickbaits such as Rebels, Rapalas, and Bombers, all in smelt colors, work very well. Trolling streamer flies is another deadly tactic for salmon. As spring turns to summer and the water warms, the trout and salmon move deep to the 70- to 120-foot range, making it necessary to use downriggers to even consider catching one of these fish. The best technique for fishing this deep consists of using a large 3- to 4-foot string of spoons referred to as a Christmas Tree. On the end of this rig is usually a 3- to 4-foot leader with a spoon or stickbaits tied to the end. This rig is trolled right on the bottom. In the North Basin, the trout and salmon can be found from Hague north to Friend's Point. Also, the areas off Rogers Rock, Anthony's Nose, and Huletts Landing down to the Mother Bunch Islands seem to hold a good quantity of trout and some salmon. In the South Basin, the trout and salmon can be found in the vicinity of Diamond Point, Tea Island, Long Island, Warner Bay, and along the drop-off near Tongue Mountain Point.

While Lake George serves up some fine summer lakers, the best fishing coincides with the smelt's spawning run, which begins shortly after ice-out (anywhere from late March to mid-April) and continues into May. Some other salmon presentations include trolling or drift-trolling offshore from smelt spawning streams, about 200 yards out, with spoons like the Miller, Sutton Flutters, or Lake Clear Wabblers with a trailing worm. Other proven lures are Mooselook Wobblers; Mooneyes in silver, gold, or copper; crankbaits

Dan Ladd with a lake trout he caught on Lake George.

such as Rapalas and Rebels in smelt colors; and J-Walkers. Early morning and late evening are the most productive hours. Fly-rodders will do well trolling Grey, Black, or Green Ghosts; Meredith Specials; Supervisors; Nine Three; Dark Montreal; Mickey Finn; or any other smeltlike streamer that leaps from the vise screaming to be fished. Fly fishermen congregate annually in late April by wading out on the Million Dollar Beach in the village of Lake George. Both laker trout and salmon can be found looking for smelt on their way to spawn in West Brook, and it's as good an excuse as any to unlimber your casting arm after a long winter. If you're so inclined to get out and cast some streamers or nymphs in this early season, take the necessary precautions to avoid hypothermia—the water temperature will be well below 50 degrees.

Just after the smelt spawning run ends, the salmon and lake trout will gradually move to slightly deeper water as the warming temperatures force them down to between 35 and 90 feet, where they are usually found in early June. This is also the time that a thermocline develops, with salmon usually being above it and lakers below it, near the bottom. Again, this is the time for downriggers or wire or lead core line. In the hottest months of July and August, the salmon may be down 50 to 90 feet, but you'll have to go even deeper for the lakers, which will be found between 100 and 180 feet. In the North Basin, the salmonids concentrate from Hague north to Friend's Point, from Rogers Rock to Indian Kettles, between Blair and Gull Bay, and from Huletts Landing to Mother Bunch Islands off Rogers Rock.

In the South Basin, the lakers and landlocked salmon are found between Diamond Point and Tea Island, between Long Island and Warner Bay, across the mouth of Dunham's Bay, and along the drop-off near Tongue Mountain Point. The areas known as the Flats and the Hill should not be overlooked. Summer fishing for salmon and lake trout is a game of odds, and like bass, electronics play a key role in locating fish. Successful anglers know that salmon are comfortable in 50- to 60-degree water but feed in 55- to 64-degree water. Lake trout seek comfort at 48 to 55 degrees and feed in a strata of 49 to 52 degrees.

In the fall, both species are fairly scattered as the water temperature is cooler and more uniform. Sweep-trolling down to 40 feet is the preferred method and offers a welcome return to light tackle as the fish, once again, are found closer to the surface. The areas around the East and West brooks in the South Basin, however, draw their share of autumn anglers.

While the fishing may be slower than in years past, the landlocked salmon of Lake George are still famous for their skyrocketing jumps and drag-testing runs. An extra rod trolled with the lure in the propeller wash, about 15 feet behind the boat, can be an effective trick if the fish aren't taking. These fish will average 2 to 3 pounds, though many between 4 and 6 pounds are taken. Once you hook one, you'll swear they are bigger. The lakers run 8 to 12 pounds, but trophy fish of 15 to 18 pounds are landed each year.

Ice Fishing

For those seeking winter sport, ice fishing has always been popular on Lake George. In fact, for some it is a way of life. While records show that Lake George has had fishable ice by the holiday season, it is usually about mid-January before anglers feel it is adequately safe. Tip-ups with minnows and suckers are standard for northerns, lakers, and salmon, but in late February, those big jack perch seem to come into their own. The game plan then changes to small minnows about 2 inches long and jigging spoons like the Swedish Pimple. Adding a perch eye always seems to increase the action, and fishing with grubs and spikes is very common. Most anglers use more than one bait on their lines.

Most anglers chasing lake trout and landlocked salmon fish deep waters. They'll put their laker setups on the bottom and run their salmon rigs at various depths, from a foot under the ice to 15 to 20 feet. Some anglers who target salmon will place two tip-ups about 5 feet apart, anticipating a school of salmon. Any deep water is fishable, and favorites include the Paulist's Fathers area in the South Basin, as well as the ice around Dome Island, Huddle Bay, the Flats and the Hill, as well as the depths of the North Basin. It should be noted that many ice fishermen fishing deep water in Lake George these days use electronics, such as flashers like the Vexilar, to find and catch fish.

For those big northern pike, try fishing the bays of Northwest, Warner, Katskill, and Dunham's, and be sure to use a steel leader. The perch beds seem to change slightly from year to year, but Canoe, Tea, and Dome islands remain pretty consistent, as does the Hogback off Long Island. Perch fishing through the ice is a social sport on Lake George, and finding the perch generally means finding the other ice fishermen—usually an easy task. Harris Bay and Log Bay are perennial favorites throughout the season, and you will see the shanty towns of both man-made structures and the portable units that have become so popular.

Charters & Boating Information

There are quite a few charter boats on Lake George piloted by knowledge-able guides. An Internet search or a trip through the local tackle shops will yield the brochures and information you will need. Charter boats furnish all equipment and generally operate from inboard/outboards ranging from 20 to 26 feet. The captains know the lake and the fishing very well, and they will teach you quite a bit while you are on the water with them.

Guides recommend trolling speeds of about 1½ miles per hour for deep fishing for lake trout and up to 5 miles per hour for landlocks near the sur-face. Trolling speeds vary with the species, depth, and lures. Advanced reser-vations are a must, as these guides are usually quite busy with repeat customers.

If you bring your own boat, you should be aware that most bays and pas-sages are zoned with a 5-mile-per-hour speed limit and that no-wake zones are prevalent in many areas. Navigation lights must be used from sunset to sunrise. Also, the following buoy code will be helpful to ensure safe travel:
- Black and white spar buoy: Marks shallow water. Do not pass between buoy and shore.
- Red buoy with red flashing light: Standard channel marker rules.
- Green buoy with green flashing light: Standard channel marker rules.
- White with quick flashing white light: Shallow water nearby.
- Red pennant: Small-craft warning of storm or high winds.

The Internet is a tremendous resource for information on Lake George, for everything from charter boats to accommodations. Here are some worth-while Web sites:
- NYS Department of Environmental Conservation: www.dec.ny.gov
- Lake George Chamber of Commerce: www.lakegeorgechamber.com
- Lake George travel and tourism sites: www.lakegeorge.com, www .visitlakegeorge.com
- NYS Outdoor Guides Association: www.nysoga.org
- Lake George Park Commission: www.lgpc.state.ny.us

About the Author

Dan Ladd is an outdoor writer from Fort Ann, New York, and has been fishing on Lake George his entire life. He published his first book, *Deer Hunting in the Adirondacks*, in 2008.

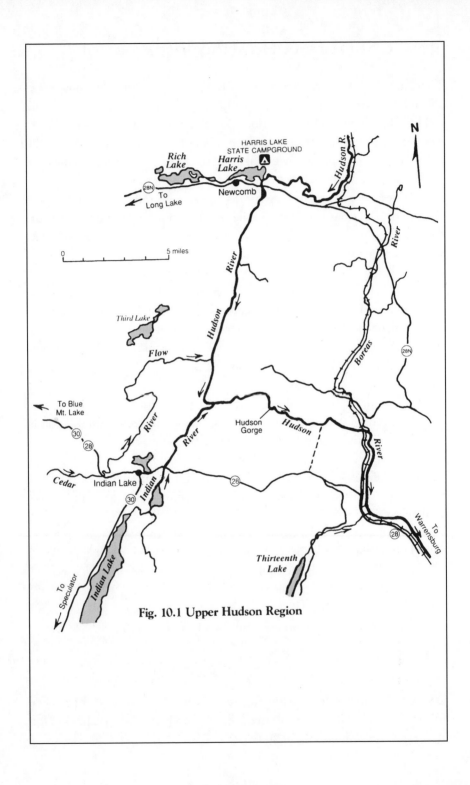

Fig. 10.1 Upper Hudson Region

CHAPTER TEN

The Beautiful Tahawus Region

Bob Zajac

T he civilization of the central Adirondacks began in 1826 with the chance meeting of an ambitious prospecting party and a controversial Abenaki Indian. David Henderson and Archibald MacIntyre hired Lewis Elijah Benedict to lead them to the iron ore deposits that had been the Native Americans' secret. They turned his fee of $1.50 and a tobacco plug into millions when they founded the Adirondack Iron Company a few years later. They called their guide Tahawus, the Indian name for Mount Marcy or "He splits the clouds." Henderson and MacIntyre left their names on the mountains above Sanford Lake, and the settlement near the original forge still bears the name Tahawus.

The industry spawned towns, and roads linking them have evolved into paved highways. The Tahawus region is accessed by I-87 and NY 28, 28N, and 30/8 and consists of portions of Essex, Hamilton, and Warren counties.

Today, lodging, campsites, food, supplies, and tackle and bait are available in Indian Lake, Speculator, Wells, North Creek, and at most exits along the Northway (I-87). The Department of Environmental Conservation (DEC) offices in Warrensburg and Ray Brook offer a variety of printed material (county specific) regarding stocking lists, guide services, and maps and are an extremely important source of information. Anglers are urged to consult the regulations, which vary considerably by location.

When to Fish the Tahawus Region

Timing your fishing trip to this region is critically important. Winter is the prodigal son among Adirondack seasons. His tantrums can be felt through April, postponing the early spring enjoyed elsewhere. On many still waters, ice-out doesn't occur until late April, and the streams are not sufficiently warmed until May. From May through June is blackfly season, and an effective repellent is a wise investment.

Peak fishing for salmonids is generally from mid-May through June. Because these species are extremely temperature sensitive, the best daytime fishing is before the heat and low-water conditions of summer. The fishing picks up again considerably in September. The fish seem to feed with urgency during the change of foliage, as if they sense the approach of the harsh winter.

Where to Go

The Hudson River begins as a trickle from Lake Tear of the Clouds. Its flow increases as it is joined by the Opalescent, Indian, and Boreas rivers. In the spring, it is a powerful river with magnum currents that demand respect when wading. From its junction with the Indian, below Blue Ledges, downstream to just below North Creek, the Hudson offers some of the area's finest fishing for brook, brown, and rainbow trout. A popular stretch of water lies adjacent to NY 28 in North Creek.

For those willing to hike, the upper Hudson offers opportunities for a distraction-free escape to a primitive wilderness area. The spectacular Blue Ledges can be reached from the east side of the river by following the North Woods Club Road outside Minerva to the DEC parking area at the Blue Ledges trailhead. Anglers willing to test their wading skills will be challenged by a variety of riffles, flats, pools, and pocket water. Waders with felt soles are recommended to ensure the best possible footing. Those who choose not to take this precaution are usually seen doing the "Tahawus shuffle," a sequence of gyrations and gestures that bears a marked resemblance to an Indian rain dance that generally results in a good soaking.

En route to the Blue Ledges, the hiker will cross the Boreas River. This stream should not be overlooked, as it can offer good trout fishing. It can be fished, upstream or down, from the crossing point and is a favorite among local anglers, especially near the still water about a mile upstream.

Below the town of North Creek, the Hudson is a series of long shallow flats with the occasional deep pool. As one proceeds south toward Glen Creek, the habitat becomes more conducive to smallmouth bass. They seem to occupy any pool offering reasonable depth.

Glen Creek enters the Hudson from the west and has some lovely, large holdover brown trout that tend to lose their natural caution during a good evening hatch. Although Glen Creek is stocked, the best fishing is near its entry with the Hudson and for a short distance upstream.

The Indian River is a productive trout fishery and can be reached by following Chain of Lakes Road north from NY 28 just east of Indian Lake village. The fishing begins just below the spillway and offers brook, brown, and rainbow trout for several miles to its junction with the Hudson. It is heavily stocked.

For those who wish to escape the crowds near the dam, the area above and below the Cedar River junction farther downstream is excellent and receives very little pressure. Caution is advised when fishing the Hudson and the Indian as their flow is regulated by the Hudson River/Black River Regulating District. Severe and sometimes sudden fluctuations in water level can occur without warning.

The Sacandaga River and its East Branch are generally accessible, as NY 30 and 8 are rarely far from their banks. The main branch from Speculator to the town of Hope is fair trout water. Augur Falls below Speculator is a photographer's delight. Better fishing is found in the Wells area, just below the Lake Algonquin dam, behind the local lumber yard, and in the pools adjacent to the parking areas along NY 30 just south of town. The falls below the dam provide increased oxygen, and the series of pools downstream have sufficient depth to sustain trout through the summer. As the river flows south toward the Sacandaga Reservoir, it becomes shallow, wider, and much warmer, creating habitat for smallmouth bass and panfish.

The best of the East Branch is found by hiking west from the Siamese Ponds Trailhead on NY 8 over Eleventh Mountain. In the cool valley below, one can enjoy solitude and brook trout. Using two cars, you can fish the 2 miles downstream to Fox Lair. The scenic Griffin Bridge area, farther down, is also worth a shot.

Other streams worth a few casts are the Jessup and Miami rivers north of Speculator, and Mill and North creeks in the township of Johnsburg, Warren County.

Be Prepared

Although not as fertile as the Catskills, this region does have an insect population that generates considerable activity from May through September. Intercepting the hatches is an iffy situation anywhere, so fly fishermen should be prepared to try subsurface techniques, including streamer fishing and upstream nymphing. The Black-Nosed Dace, Mickey Finn, and Woolly Bugger streamers (numbers 4 through 8), and Gold-Ribbed Hare's Ear and stone fly nymphs (numbers 8 through 14), are consistent producers.

During July and August, feeding activity is generally confined to early morning and late evening, when the water is cool. Exceptions occur during cold, overcast periods when the rivers escape the heat of the sun. It is noteworthy that on occasion, rainbows can be "pounded up" by fishing pocket water with high-floating dry flies such as the popular Wulff patterns. These fish seem to prefer the faster currents and can be quite cooperative with this method.

Fly tackle for fishing the streams requires a rod of 7 to 8½ feet for a 5 or 6 weight line, enabling the angler to present a variety of fly sizes by varying leader length and tippet size. The length of rod is usually a personal choice, with the shorter rod favored for smaller streams.

The spin fisherman should be appropriately equipped with light tackle capable of handling 6-pound test and a variety of spinners and spoons in the ¼-ounce range. The Mepps Spinner, Mepps Minnow, Panther Martin, Phoebe, and Little Cleo are all very effective. A favorite bait-fishing technique is working a minnow or worm on a number 6 hook below a split shot through the riffles and into the depths of the pools.

Indian Lake

For those who prefer lake fishing, Indian Lake is highly recommended. Located in Hamilton County, this 4,500-acre impoundment offers beautiful scenery, easy access, and a variety of fish. Canoe and boat rentals are readily available, and there is a state boat launch. State campsites are located on shore and on several islands as well.

A boat cuts through the early morning mist as an angler
baits up a hook in the shadow of Tahawus.

A season on Indian Lake begins in May with northern pike fishing. Techniques include trolling large spoons close to shore and still-fishing large minnows or suckers below a bobber in the shallows. The Lake Abanaki area adjacent to Indian Lake near Sabael is popular and produces northerns in the 4- to 10-pound range. There is also a smelt run in May where Squaw Brook enters Indian Lake on the west side.

Beginning in June, and continuing through the summer, anglers are busy casting for smallmouth bass that can reach the 2- to 3-pound class. Whatever your choice of lures, current or vintage, will be fine, especially on the south and west sides of the lake along several islands. As with many constructed lakes, the bottom is composed of a variety of structure, which attracts game fish.

The rock ledges along the east shore are an indication of good water and deserve considerable attention. In the early morning, and again later in the evening, top-water plugs provide exciting bass action, with northern pike adding an occasional explosive surprise.

The best area for landlocked salmon and lake trout is the north end of Indian Lake, just above the dam, where the water covers the original streambed. Standard trolling techniques will take the occasional fish, but trout fishing has fallen off in recent years because of the severe fluctuations in water level that are due to dam releases in the spring and fall.

In addition, Indian Lake has an abundance of perch, bullhead, crappie, and other panfish available to the angler armed with worms and small children. It is an ideal spot for a family vacation.

Thirteenth Lake and Other Ponds

There is a special magic associated with brook trout fishing in an Adirondack pond. The spectacular view of close and distant mountains, along with the quiet pace, can be hypnotic, until broken by a rising fish. Thirteenth Lake, Kibby, Peaked Mountain, Puffer, and the Siamese ponds in Warren County are typical of the region. Hamilton County offers Terrell, Owl, and others, such as Mason Lake, with its added bonus of brown trout. Spin fishermen generally cast bait, spinners, or small spoons, while locals, a generation older, cling to the tradition of trolling a worm behind a Lake Clear Wabbler. These techniques are on the decline in recent years because of the DEC's efforts to protect these fragile ecosystems.

In many of these ponds, anglers are prohibited from using live bait of any kind as the present population of trout is the product of countless dollars and hours of effort required to reclaim these fisheries. Shamefully, a number of other ponds have been lost to coarse fish inadvertently dumped from the minnow buckets of violators.

In the late 1870s, Henry Barton began mining garnet in the Gore Mountain area. Ore containing these ruby-colored crystals was abundantly embedded in the anorthosite crust of nearby mountains as well. While the mountains overlooking Thirteenth Lake bear the scars of man's lust for a precious stone, anglers canoeing Thirteenth Lake can discover other jewels: brook trout, brown trout, and remnant landlocked salmon.

Thirteenth Lake is a narrow ribbon of water, 2 miles in length, resting between Hour Pond Mountain and Balm of Gilead Mountain. It is easily accessible by car and can be reached via Thirteenth Lake Road, which meets NY 28 just west of North Creek.

At the parking area, you will note DEC posters defining current special regulations. Legal size and creel limits may vary from year to year, but Thirteenth Lake has been "artificials only" since the DEC reclaimed and stocked it in 1972. Big browns and big brookies are an elusive challenge; the landlocked salmon program, which once bordered on phenomenal, is currently under review by the DEC.

Perhaps the most common method of fishing the lake is the slow troll from a canoe or small boat, which allows you to peacefully cover the water and enjoy the glorious mountain scenery. A small nymph (number 10 to 14) trailing about 60 feet behind is generally productive throughout the season, but anglers should also be aware of the existence of other opportunities. The fish seem to congregate where Peaked Mountain Brook enters the lake about ½ mile down on the west shore. A smelt streamer can be deadly both in this area and at the far (south) end of the lake, where beaver have dammed Buck Meadow Flow.

The warmer temperatures of spring stimulate insect activity that continues until the summer's heat becomes oppressive. Although trolling may remain a part of the game plan, it is now time to have a second rod ready in anticipation of dry-fly activity. Opportunities are numerous when the lake is calm, as risers can be seen from a considerable distance, but even the slightest breeze will ruffle the surface, making the telltale rings difficult to distinguish even at close range.

Midday opportunities occur, but at the mercy of the breezes. Shortly after 5, though, the winds often settle down for the evening. Trout now cruise just under the surface in groups, or pods, selectively dining on the insect du jour.

Fish rise to Callibaetis, a size 16 gray mayfly, but the importance of this hatch is generally overshadowed by the presence of caddis, in various sizes, that are usually on the water at the same time in greater numbers. The small, mothlike caddis are seen in several life stages: resting on the surface just after hatching, hovering above the water during their mating flights, and dipping to the surface and depositing their eggs. The most common size is a number 16, and again, the fish seem to be more selective to size than specific dressings. Caddis emergers are also productive during these hatches.

The Elk Hair, Henryville, and skittering caddis patterns are equally effective, but the most difficult aspects of fishing the surface are not fly patterns, but approach and presentation. The most efficient method of approach during these "glassed out," surface conditions is to stop paddling a goodly distance away and quietly coast to the fish, or to get into position and wait until their feeding direction brings them to you.

These fish are easily spooked, and the complexity of the situation is compounded by the fact that, unlike stream fishing, where the quarry maintains a position in a feeding lane, fish in still waters cruise the surface. The constant

Bob Zajac with a fine trout taken in the Tahawus region. At least a half dozen good trout streams converge in this upper Hudson area.

movement of these fish requires that the angler determine direction, anticipate where the next rise will occur, and have the fly waiting there as the fish
approaches. Light tippets, long casts, small flies, perfect timing, and flawless
presentation are the components of success on any Adirondack still water.
Taking fish under these conditions provides a great challenge but even
greater rewards.

In May, June, and again in September, the hatches can present more
challenges, or more frustrations, as the lake changes its menu. The caddis and
mayfly activity continues, but careful observation will yield that the fish may
now be stuffing themselves with diptera. These mosquito-like chironomids
are preferred in their pupal state. Just before hatching, the pupae rest suspended in the surface film, invisible to the angler, who may believe that the
fish are rising for no apparent reason. A size 16 imitation of these delicate
minutiae will produce if the angler maintains discipline.

The degree of difficulty increases dramatically here—the tactics are the
same for the caddis and mayfly hatches, except you cannot see the fly you are
fishing. You strike when there is a rise where you believe your fly to be. This
is postdoctoral fly-fishing and a supreme challenge. It requires perseverance,
a bit of masochism, and a little Zen.

In early June, brown-bodied, gray-winged hexagenia mayflies, of
Homeric proportions, emerge at the south end of the lake. The hatch usually occurs during the noon–3 period, allowing the angler to intercept it ca-
sually. These insects are a hook size 8 2XL and demand attention. They will
occasionally flutter and fall clumsily back to the water, bringing slashing rises.
This is the hatch that brings the big fish up, and a good hex hatch is a spec-
tacle of sight and noise that raises the hair on the back of your neck and
leaves memories indelibly etched in your mind.

A personal muse: I have witnessed blackbirds and swallows pluck these
huge insects from the air and struggle with them in flight to the shoreline
alders for a supposed feast. Sometimes the bird comes out . . . sometimes the
mayfly comes out! Big bugs . . . ayuh.

Although wading is possible at the southern end, more area can be covered from a canoe. Long casts with nymph imitations stripped back will
bring fish, but the greatest sport is to be had with the dry fly. It is essential
that presentations are gently placed ahead of cruising fish, allowed to rest,
and twitched slightly if necessary to induce a rise. Again, these fish have
shown selectivity to size more than pattern, and large Wulffs, hair wings, and
spider types such as the Grey Fox Variant all have their day.

During the heat of July and August, the hatches subside considerably. Although there is generally a hatch just at dark, most fish are taken during the day by deep trolling. Long rods are an asset for trolling but are more important for dry-fly fishing from a boat or canoe. The additional length of an 8½- or 9-foot rod allows the seated angler to increase casting distance by simple laws of physics. Any good single-action fly reel with a light, smooth drag will do nicely. Line weight for trolling is not an issue, but trying to push a large fly, in windy conditions, during the hex hatch, will require a 6- or 7-weight rod. For the more delicate presentations of smaller flies, an 8½-footer for a 5- or 6-weight line is about right. Leader length for dry-fly fishing the ponds should start at about 12 feet.

Two-year-old brown and rainbow trout are now stocked here, and they average 12 to 16 inches upon arrival. Holdovers are common. The brook trout of Thirteenth Lake range from 10 to 18-plus inches, and a girthy 14-incher would be considered a lovely fish. The beautiful brookie is the all-American boy that provides us with a link to a great era of Adirondack angling gone by and with a symbol of our obligation to preserve these fragile environs for the future.

About the Author

Bob Zajac is a freelance writer who lives in Guilderland, New York, with his wife, son, and daughter. He is a retired administrator with the NYS Office of Vocational Rehabilitation and has been a frequent contributor to the *Atlantic Salmon Journal* and *Eastern Woods and Waters,* and he is editor-at-large for an online magazine for Atlantic salmon. He has also written and edited numerous chapters of books for Northeast Sportsman's Press/Stackpole Books. He spends much of the summer chasing Atlantic salmon on Quebec rivers.

CHAPTER ELEVEN

Washington and Saratoga Counties: Fishing the Eastern Slopes

Greg Cuda

Saratoga and Washington counties rest at the foothills of the Adirondack and Green mountains. Despite encroachment from southern population centers, these counties have maintained their rural character with rolling hills, farmscapes, and distant mountain vistas. Many lakes, ponds, rivers, and creeks offer nearly endless angling opportunities for both warm- and cold-water fish species. There are many quality choices available to the angler, but the undisputed gem of the region is the fabled Battenkill.

The Battenkill River

The Battenkill's reputation as a trout stream owes as much to the residents in the valley as it does to the actual fishing experience. Over the years, the watershed has attracted a number of notable artists, authors, and anglers.

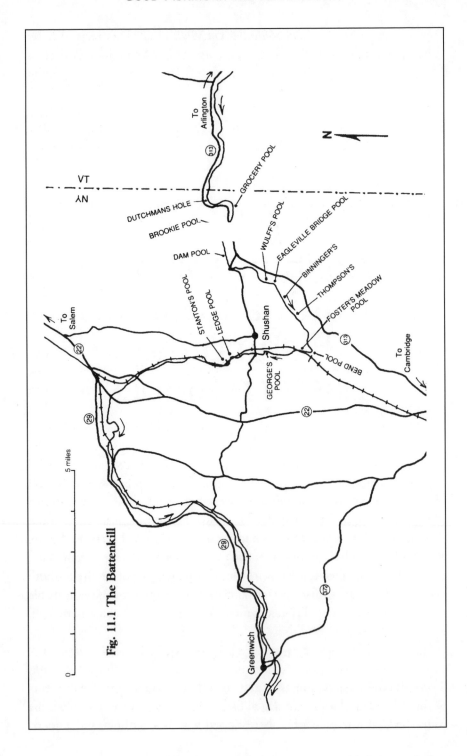

Fig. 11.1 The Battenkill

During the 1940s, four *Saturday Evening Post* illustrators resided here: Norman Rockwell, Meade Schaeffer, George Hughes, and John Atherton. Many of Rockwell's well-known images were painted using local people and scenes as models. During the same period, in nearby North Hoosic, New York, Grandma Moses was capturing timeless scenes that have not changed to this day. Celebrated landscape artist Ogden Pleissner lived in the valley from 1977 to 1983. Some of Pleissner's original artwork can be seen in Manchester, Vermont's, American Museum of Fly Fishing.

Lee Wulff, author, angler, artist, and filmmaker, lived on the banks of the river in Shushan, New York, from 1940 to 1960. Arguably the best-known figure in angling history, Wulff was also a conservationist who was quoted as saying, "a game fish is too valuable and precious to be caught only once." A testament to his legacy is now in place on the Battenkill. Several years after his death, New York implemented a "catch-and-release, artificial lure only" area on the waters of his former home.

Angling authors have resided in the valley extending back to the 19th century, including George Washington Bethune, John Harrington Kean, Charles Orvis, and Mary Orvis Marbury. More recent angling books have been penned by John Atherton, Craig Woods, and Tom Rosenbauer. Anyone with more than a passing interest in the river must read John Merwin's book titled simply *The Battenkill*.

The upper river in Vermont flows through an area of limestone bedrock, which causes the water to become mildly alkaline. Feeder streams enter the river from both the Green and Taconic mountains. The different geologies of these mountain ranges cause the Battenkill to exhibit both freestone and limestone characteristics. Numerous springs and cold-water tributaries add to the flow before the Battenkill reaches New York. As a result, most of the river in New York seldom rises above 70 degrees Fahrenheit. Even today, the Battenkill maintains its tree-lined canopy for much of its length, which further contributes to its temperature stability. The result of the Battenkill's plentiful cool alkaline water is a self-sustaining brook trout population that is rare in a river of its size outside the state of Maine.

When fishing the Battenkill, you will be taken back in time. The setting is much like it was when Grandma Moses captured the scenery during the 1940s. Covered bridges still span the river, dirt roads cross the county, and farming is still the largest industry.

The Battenkill is not an easy river to fish. Despite many anglers' claims to the contrary, the fish are there. Studies by New York State Department of

Environmental Conservation (DEC) show the Battenkill has one of the highest rates of natural reproduction of any river in the state. In addition to the wild brown and brook trout, the state stocks approximately 20,000 brown trout in the river. Deceptively swift currents, clear water, sporadic insect hatches, and a lack of obvious cover conspire against the angler. The key ingredients for successful dry-fly fishing on this river are patience; a long, fine leader; extremely careful wading; and casting down and across to specific targets.

The Battenkill in New York's upper river extends from the Vermont state line downstream 4.4 miles to the Eagleville covered bridge. This reach is managed as a catch-and-release artificial-lure-only fishery and is stocked with two-year-old brown trout, but wild brown and brook trout are also present. Special trout-fishing regulations can be found on the DEC Web site (www.dec.ny.gov) or in the state's fishing regulations handbook, available wherever fishing licenses are sold. Due to brook trout's preference for cold water, these native fish can be found anywhere an inflow of cold water joins the Battenkill, including creek mouths and spring holes. Access along New York's upper Battenkill is excellent, as the river has extensive public fishing rights (PFRs) along its banks. These easements allow anglers to walk the riverbank within 33 feet of the water. Details of New York's PFRs are available on the DEC Web site. Below Eagleville the river is managed under New York's general trout fishing regulations, but the fishing can be as good as, and often better than, the special-regulations area.

The upper Battenkill can be accessed in several locations, including the NY 313 rest area near the Vermont state line. The PFR section starts here, so you can walk the banks to search for good holding water. You will often see anglers' cars parked along NY 313 where the road crosses the river. It has earned its popularity for good reason, as fish hold along the ledge rock above and below the NY 313 bridge. Hickory Hill Road follows the river on its north bank. Most of this property is posted, but park on the road shoulder and look for PFR signs to gain access to the stream bank. Heading downstream, you will soon cross over Camden Valley Creek. Fishing at its mouth can be a good place to find brook trout during the summer trico hatch. Just downstream is the famed Spring Hole, located where the County Route 61 iron bridge crosses the river. Old-timers speak of a tackle shop that was located on the bank at the pool's edge. The Spring Hole is still a popular location due to its healthy population of brook trout and the occasional large brown. Located downstream is Wulff's Pool, where Lee Wulff's former home still overlooks the water. The Battenkill in this section had become over-

GREG CUDA

A nice Battenkill brown trout.

widened and shallow. To improve the habitat in this reach, the Clearwater Chapter of Trout Unlimited has completed a geomorphic restoration project here. This pool is most easily reached by walking upstream from the angler parking area on Eagleville Road. Farther downstream, the covered bridge at Eagleville represents the end of the catch-and-release artificial-lure area.

The next river crossing is the County Route 64 bridge, known locally as Pook's Bridge. There are several parking areas here, all privately owned and maintained by local farmers. One pull-off has a sign requesting river users to keep the area clean and to not park in the fields, lest the area be posted. This is good advice while parking anywhere along the river. To fish the area between the bridges means a long walk or float; however, there are several large pools in this area that make the effort worthwhile.

Anglers looking for solitude will find it below the village of Shushan, where the river takes a 4-mile detour away from any roads. The Battenkill Railroad follows the stream, and the pools are named after the four trestles that traverse the river. Due to liberal stocking by the state, good fishing can be found at the Rexleigh covered bridge, but just downstream the river becomes quite wide, and anglers should choose other options. Farther downstream, the DEC maintains an anglers parking area where the river passes under NY 22. Due to depth and cover, the pools below this area tend to be more productive than those above. The riverbank below NY 22 can be reached where it skirts NY 29 or at the bridges in East Greenwich and Battenville. Though good fishing can be found in this stretch, the lower river tends to warm significantly during the heat of the summer (July and August), making it advisable to choose other angling options rather than subject the trout to undue stress.

The hatches on the Battenkill emerge, surprisingly, at nearly the same time, or perhaps a week or two later, as those of the famed Catskill Rivers to the south. The star of the Battenkill's spring season is the hendrickson (*Ephemeralla subvaria*) mayfly. There are other bugs about, such a blue quills, caddis flies, and stone flies, but it is the hendrickson hatch, which starts to emerge at the end of April, that brings the fish to the surface, including some very large trout that don't show themselves at other times of the year. The hatch can be maddening, however, as the water is often high and cold due to spring rains and snowmelt in the distant Vermont Mountains. The surface of the river is often covered with insects, with not a rising trout in sight. In these instances, you can be sure the fish are gorging below the surface, so nymph fishing is in order. Once the hatch gets rolling, you may want to stick around for the evening spinner fall, as the trout are sure to rise to the helpless mayflies. By mid-June, the early season hatches are over, and the best dry-fly fishing occurs at dusk. It can be tough to figure out exactly what is happening in the brief minutes before darkness sets in. Emergers, duns, spinners, and caddis flies can all be on the water at the same time, and it is challenging to figure out what the fish are taking. Favorite mayfly imitations on the Battenkill often include parachute patterns, which can imitate a dun or spinner and still allow the angler to see them in the failing light.

An angling mentor once said that mayflies hatch at the most comfortable time of the day. Following suit, as summer progresses, the hatches on the river switch over to morning. The diminutive trico hatch starts in mid-July and can continue through the first frosts of September. The flies, typically size 22 or 24, are heaviest near the New York State line but can be found throughout the river system. Tricos usually hatch at night, and it is the morning spinner fall that brings the trout to the surface. To time it correctly, anglers should be on the water before the air temperature hits 70 degrees (Fahrenheit). Look for swarms of tiny flies above the riffle sections of the river. The spinner fall can sometimes be dramatic and briefly bring up every

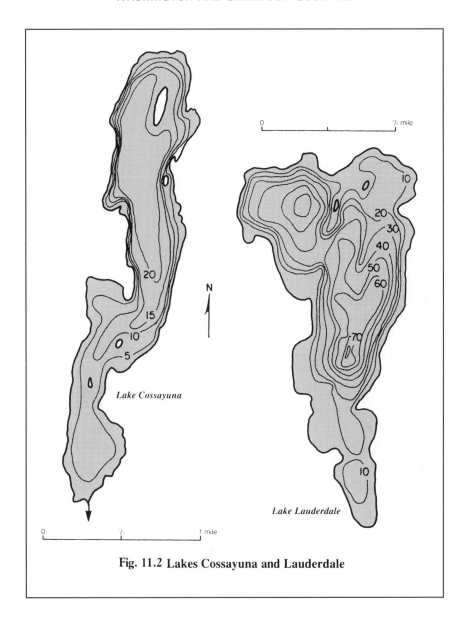

Fig. 11.2 Lakes Cossayuna and Lauderdale

trout in the river. More typically, the fish can rise sporadically for over an hour. This is challenging fishing requiring long 6x or 7x leaders, with gentle presentations and careful wading. Pick out a single fish and watch for its rhythm. Most often a trout will rise two or three times in quick succession and then rest. Be sure your fly is on that fish's nose when it decides to come up. Mid-September brings the advent of the blue-winged olive hatch. The BWOs can be found anywhere in the river system. To intercept these small size 18 or 20 mayflies, it is best to be on the river in the late afternoon during cloudy and overcast days. Chances are good that you will be fighting a stiff breeze and skinny water. Using subsurface flies is difficult as you are more likely to catch fallen leaves than trout. If the trout refuse your dry flies, an emerger in the surface film can be effective. At times it seems the fish sense the coming of winter and can be greedy in their feeding.

Due to the sporadic nature of most Battenkill hatches, anglers intent on dry-fly fishing may spend a lot of time on the bank in search of rising fish. Many experienced anglers have better luck fishing wet flies down and across, often with two or three flies. Generic wet-fly patterns such as the Soft Hackles, Hare's Ears, and a Battenkill favorite, the Breadcrust, can be effective. Fish the fast water just as it enters the slow pools, swinging the fly across and down on a tight line. There is no mistaking the take while using this technique. Though the best time to use this method is early morning, preferably before the sun hits the water, wet flies can be effective any time of the day. Some anglers target larger fish by using streamers. The patterns developed by famed fly-tier Lew Oatman, including the Shushan Postmaster and Battenkill Shiner, are still effective with olive and black Woolly Buggers, also found to be reliable. Anglers who prefer to use a spinning rod will have the best luck when the water is on the rise after a rainfall or at dawn and dusk.

It is important to mention that the Battenkill is a favorite for floaters as well as anglers. Warm summer weekend days can bring out an extremely heavy Kevlar hatch—a flotilla of devices including tubes, kayaks, and canoes. Several liveries are located in the valley, and many tourists as well as local residents use the river as a cool refuge from the summer heat. The area with heaviest traffic is from the Vermont state line downstream to the village of Shushan. An angler would be wise to be off the water shortly after the trico spinner fall and head upriver or down. This is also a good time to explore some of the area's other angling opportunities.

Battenkill River Tributaries

There are several Battenkill tributaries that are outstanding fisheries in their own right. White Creek, in the town of Salem, runs cold and clear throughout the summer. Though it is a small stream, it demands stealth and skill to catch any fish at all. The creek holds a good population of wild brook and brown trout, with the state supplementing their numbers with an annual stocking of 1,300 brown trout. This creek is an important spawning tributary for the Battenkill, and efforts are being made to protect and improve the habitat by the Adirondack and Clearwater Chapters of Trout Unlimited, with help from the Batten Kill Watershed Alliance and the U.S. Fish and Wildlife Service. Anglers looking to catch brook trout can explore Camden Valley Creek. Cool springs feed the headwaters of the creek, making for ideal habitat for the native fish.

Hoosic River Tributaries

Southern Washington County offers many small tributary streams that feed that the Hoosic River, with nearly all of them holding trout. Wild brown and rainbow are the most prevalent species of trout found here, but brook trout can be found in the upland sections of most streams. Flowing south out of the village of Cambridge, New York, and paralleling NY 22 for much of its length, the Owl Kill is the area's largest stream and receives some supplemental stocking, while White Creek, Center White Creek, and Little White Creek are all worth exploring. Small stream trout are more likely to rise to a well-presented dry fly than fish on the larger rivers. This makes the area's creeks a good option at those times before or after the hatches are expected on the Battenkill. These streams tend to run cooler than the large rivers as well, so good fishing can be found in the heat of the summer.

Mettawee River

Though often overshadowed by the Battenkill, the Mettawee River is a fine stream in its own right. Originating in the mountains of Vermont just outside of Dorset, the small stream picks up innumerable small feeders to become a sizable river by the time it reaches the New York border near Granville. The character of this section of river is fast riffles running between the long, slow pools, with several waterfalls along its length. Both browns and rainbows reproduce naturally here, and New York supplements the population by stocking both species. Details on all stocking in Washington and Saratoga counties are available from the DEC Web site, on its Fish Stocking List.

The Indian River is a productive tributary to the Mettawee. With its headwaters in Vermont, the Indian follows the Green Mountain state's tradition of naming anything larger than a trickle a river. This small stream with a big name holds a healthy population of brown and rainbow trout. The

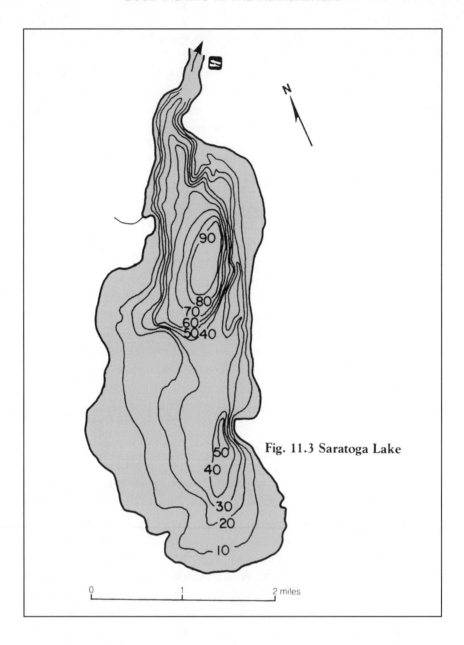

Fig. 11.3 Saratoga Lake

lower reaches of the creek meander through open meadows where beavers occasionally change the character of the stream with their busy work. Alternatively, there is a roiling pocket water stretch where the Indian enters New York near West Pawlet that has proven to be productive.

Poultney River

The Poultney River forms the border between New York and Vermont along much of its length at the northern border of Washington County. The character of the river is quite dramatic, with large waterfalls interspersed with long, slow-moving pools. The river flows away from the road in many sections and does not give away its secrets easily. The Poultney is popular with local spin and bait fishermen.

Hudson River

Separating Saratoga and Washington counties is the famed Hudson River. Below the waterfall in Troy, New York, the river is rich with a huge variety of fish, including striped bass, shad, and sturgeon, along with freshwater bass and pike. Above the dam, the target species for most anglers is the smallmouth bass. The river has suffered much abuse from industrial pollution over the years. In fact, due to contamination of PCBs (Polychlorinated biphenyls, a chemical released into the Hudson by General Electric between the 1940s and the 1970s), large sections of the river are being managed as a catch-and-release fishery. What has emerged is an outstanding but underutilized smallmouth bass fishery. New York maintains a boat launch in Schuylerville that allows access to a particularly productive stretch of river. The Battenkill enters just above the launch, and the smallmouth fishing can be quite good on the Hudson and even into the lower Battenkill. During low-water periods, anglers who prefer wading can access the river below the diversion dam near the Champlain Canal lock in Schuylerville. Additional Hudson River boat launches can be found along Spier Falls Road in the town of Corinth. The river in this section flows between dams, can feel quite remote in places, and is a good place to enjoy fishing from a canoe or small boat. The bass can be plentiful here but run smaller than the downstream reaches.

Cold-Water Fishing

Saratoga County offers cold-water anglers several opportunities, with the Kayaderosseras being the largest and most popular stream. Most often referred to as the Kaydeross Creek, the river is primarily a brown trout fishery and receives and annual stocking of approximately twelve thousand fish. The trout fishing begins in the village of Ballston Spa and continues upstream into the town of Corinth. The Kaydeross has some good early season stone fly hatches named snow flies for their willingness to hatch while snowbanks still line the river. Two varieties of stone flies, sizes 12 and 16, begin to emerge on late March afternoons and remain a fishable hatch well into April. The Kaydeross above the first railroad bridge in Ballston Spa is open to angling year-round, so if the weather cooperates and the river is not too high, dry-fly fishing can be had in late March. Along with the standard complement of eastern mayfly hatches, the river produces a green drake mayfly hatch around Memorial Day each spring. By this time of year, most other anglers have headed to the lakes or other pursuits, and fine fishing can be had in near solitude. Look for a good number of these giant insects below the village of Rock City Falls. There is angler parking areas in many locations along the creek, including Creek Road in Factory Village, Geiser Road in Milton Center, Rock City Road in Rock City Falls, NY 29 and South Creek Road in Middle Grove, Holmes Road in South Corinth, and Bockes Road, among others. The lower river from South Creek Road in Middle Grove to Ballston Spa is wider and therefore more compatible with fly-fishing. Bait fishermen can have good success anywhere along the Kaydeross, but many specialize in the willow-choked upper reaches of the creek. Below Ballston Spa, the creek is popular with canoers and kayakers. This reach of river is primarily a warm-water fishery and is closed to angling from March 16 until the opening of walleye season in May to protect the spawning fish.

The Glowegee Creek is a feeder stream to the Kaydeross and is also stocked with brown trout. The upper reaches of this creek, like most of the streams in northern Saratoga County, also hold brook trout. Access on the Kaydeross and Glowegee is good as both streams have extensive public fishing rights.

Gregarious anglers may find Geyser Brook to their liking. Flowing through the Saratoga Spa State Park, the creek receives a very public trout stocking. The DEC promotes the event as an opportunity to educate the next generation of anglers, and many families take part in the festivities.

Flowing through the town of Gansevoort, New York, another lesser-known but enjoyable stream is the Snook Kill. New York State maintains public fishing easements on this stream, and it is stocked with brown trout. Access for the stream can be found on Dimmick Road, the Wilton Gansevoort Road, and along County Route 32. The Snook Kill is popular just after the stocking trucks arrive, but anglers who come to visit it later in the season will most likely have the creek to themselves.

Still-Water Fishing

Washington County has several opportunities for trout fishing in still water. Dead Pond, located at the corner of NY 22 and CR 61, is annually stocked with two thousand brown trout. This small lake is deep and can provide anglers with the occasional surprise in the form of large holdover fish. Along with trout, Dead Pond supports a healthy population of bass, sunfish, and crappie. For anglers willing to step off the beaten path and do some hiking, there are two ponds high above Lake George's eastern shore that support trout. Bumps Pond is small and holds brook trout, while Fishbrook Pond has a population of rainbow trout. Fishbrook is larger and farther from the road, and produces correspondingly larger fish. The pond has several lean-to camping sites for anglers who desire to spend a few days exploring the area. The trailhead for both ponds is at Dacy Clearing. To reach the trailhead from NY 149 (east), turn left onto Buttermilk Falls Road (which becomes Sly Pond Road), bear left on Shelving Rock Road, and park in the DEC hikers' lot. The trail is well marked and leads to both ponds. The climb is quite steep in places, but you will be rewarded with spectacular views of Lake George for your efforts.

Hedges, Lauderdale, and Cassayuna lakes offer good quality warm-water fisheries. Access is difficult as all the land around the lakes is privately owned, with the exception of a Washington County–run park on Lauderdale. Car-top boats can be launched at the park.

Saratoga County's still-water fisheries primarily offer warm-water species. Saratoga Lake is the largest and most heavily fished but is also very productive. The lake offers a long list of species, including largemouth and smallmouth bass, walleye, northern pike, yellow perch, sunfish, and crappie. The state maintains a boat launch at the north end of the lake just off NY 9P. Several private marinas allow the launching of boats from a trailer as well. Saratoga Lake, located just outside Saratoga Springs, New York, is 8 miles long, 2 miles wide, and 90 feet deep. As the water warms in the summer, the lake becomes very weedy. The use of top water lures can be productive for bass when fished along the weed edges at dawn and dusk. Many anglers fish the weed beds with rubber worms or spinnerbaits set up to be weedless. Saratoga Lake is popular with ice fishermen as well.

In the same watershed as Saratoga Lake is Lake Lonely. Access is limited to the Lake Lonely Boat Livery on Crescent Road in the town of Saratoga, but the livery offers boat launching and small-boat rentals. This comparatively lightly fished body of water can produce fine bass fishing. Ballston Lake, narrow and 3½ miles long, has a well-deserved reputation for producing trophy smallmouth bass and northern pike. Canoes can be launched at the public fishing dock at the north end of the lake on Outlet Road. No public boat launch exists to accommodate trailed boats, but the Good Times Restaurant on Lake Shore Road allows boaters to launch for a fee. Round Lake is a tenth of the size of Saratoga Lake but holds a good population of both bass and pike. Access for Round Lake is on NY 9 in the village of the same name.

In northern Saratoga County, New York State operates Moreau Lake State Park, including a campground, hiking trails, and a swimming beach. Rowboats can be rented at the campground, and slow trolling under oars is a popular fishing technique on the lake. Moreau Lake has a five-fish limit, it has no closed season for trout, and it is open to ice fishermen.

As you can see, there are countless fishing opportunities in Washington and Saratoga counties, from warm-water lakes and ponds to smallmouth bass on the Hudson to world-class trout fishing on the Battenkill. Along with the larger lakes and the Mohawk River, there are many smaller bodies of water, streams, and creeks waiting to be explored—all in a setting that Grandma Mosses would find familiar if she were alive today.

About the Author

Greg Cuda is a founding member and chairman of the Batten Kill Watershed Alliance (BKWA) and a past president of the Clearwater Chapter of Trout Unlimited. The BKWA was formed to promote good stewardship of the Battenkill River in both New York and Vermont. He is an administrator for Saratoga Bridges, an organization serving the needs of people with disabilities and their families. Greg resides in Saratoga Springs, New York, with his wife, Susan.

CHAPTER TWELVE

Exciting Fishing Just North of the Thruway

Ron Kolodziej

Wayfaring anglers using the New York State Thruway as a jumping-off point will find top-notch opportunities not only within the Adirondack Park Blue Line, but in the peripheral areas as well. Let's consider one such area.

Spread out your map of New York State and locate Amsterdam, just west of Albany. Now draw a line due north to the community of Edinburg, on the shores of Great Sacandaga Lake. From there extend your line due west to Alder Creek and then due south along NY 12 to Utica. Now trace a line over the Thruway back to where you started. If you fish anywhere within this roughly rectangular area, you're never much more than 35 to 40 miles from the Thruway, but you have access to some 1,500 square miles of superb fishing opportunities, ranging from record-breaking northerns to bragging-sized brook trout.

Great Sacandaga Lake

Let's begin our odyssey at Great Sacandaga Lake on the eastern edge of our chosen area. Created in 1930 as a flood-control impoundment by construction of a large earthen dam at Conklingville on the Sacandaga River, this lake produced a world-record northern pike in 1940, caught by Peter Dubuc. It was a magnificent 51½-inch, 46-pound, 2-ounce fish that held the world record for almost 40 years. Although eventually bested by European pike, it still lays claim to the North American record for that species.

The halcyon days for Sacandaga Reservoir, as it was then called, lasted through the late 1950s and early 1960s. By that time the richly fertile farmlands and swamplands inundated by the impoundment had leached the last of their nutrients into the water. Fluctuating water levels and a general lack of forage fish caused a gradual but perceptible decline in the fishery. It eventually stabilized and still offers great year-round fishing for northern, walleye, yellow perch, and bass in season. Thanks to the efforts of the all-volunteer Great Sacandaga Lake Fisheries Federation, which has conducted a very successful trout-stocking program in the lake for the past 20 years, trout fishing has become nothing short of spectacular in Great Sacandaga. The stockings have been primarily of rainbows, but a substantial number of browns and even some landlocked salmon have been released. In May 2009, the group's 25th anniversary, it celebrated another impressive milestone by stocking its 100,000th trout in the lake.

Conventional fishing methods for the above species will work well on Great Sacandaga. Drift-fishing with Lake Clear Wabblers and a trailer hook baited with a night crawler or minnow is a good, easy, productive technique for walleye and perch. Cabela's Walleye Wobble jigs in fluorescent red and green have also proved to be excellent on the lake's walleyes. Drift-fished live bait can also work well on that species. Sacandaga's smallmouths respond well to crawfish, hellgrammites, and minnows, but also to a variety of artificials, such as Mepps spinners and various crankbaits. The average Great Sacandaga walleye will weigh in the 1- to 2-pound range, with 6- to 7-pounders being taken annually. Smallmouths will also average 1 to 2 pounds, with occasional 5-pounders. Largemouths, though not as common as smallmouths, can also range to 5 pounds. Rainbow trout can be caught with spinner/worm combos, streamers, and bucktails or any other traditional rainbow lures. Rainbows in the lake have exceeded 6 pounds, though the average is nearer 18 to 20 inches.

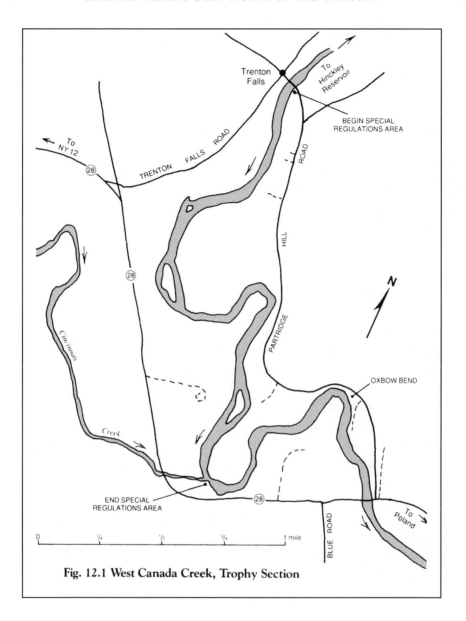

Fig. 12.1 West Canada Creek, Trophy Section

Browns weighing up to 5 pounds have also been reported.

Over the years, a number of big 8- to 12-pound catfish have also been taken in the lake, though the reader is cautioned against visiting Great Sacandaga specifically for that species. They're uncommon at best, and it's not known what their population level is or how they came to be in the lake.

Escape from area farm ponds appears to be one plausible explanation, though there are others, including intentional introduction by anglers wishing to perhaps "spice up" their fishing choices.

If Sacandaga's big northerns are your quarry, plan on shore fishing with big minnows since few really big fish are taken by other methods, such as casting or trolling. Trophy-hunting pike aficionados stake out a piece of accessible shoreline—generally in the lake's shallower southwest basin between the communities of Mayfield and Broadalbin—and rig up light saltwater or heavy-duty freshwater gear baited with 12- to 15-inch suckers. Then it's a waiting game. Prime time is May and early June when water levels are high and the northerns are still in the shallower, flooded portions of the shoreline before, during, and immediately after spawning. The same method will work if you're fishing from a boat, but, of course, you'll then be casting your bait toward shore rather than out from it. If trolling is your preferred method, use large Dardevles in traditional red and white, or jointed Rapalas, Rebels, Thundersticks, Yo-Zuris, or similar lures in perch or other natural finishes. Depending on time of day, weather, water conditions, and depth, your best trolling speeds will be between 1½ and 2½ miles per hour. For the most part, you'll be trolling water less than 10 feet deep and somewhat tight to the shoreline. Planer boards can help keep you "in the zone."

Boat launches are available at Northville on the Sacandaga River, at the Northampton Beach Campsite just south of Northville, in the town of Day in the northeast arm, and near the village of North Broadalbin. These are state-operated, free facilities, but commercial launches can also be found liberally scattered around the lake. However, shorebound anglers on Great Sacandaga need not feel left out. Access to good shore-fishing areas is readily available along much of the lake's 125-mile shoreline. I recommend the areas around Northville and Batchellerville Bridge, along much of the Sacandaga River paralleled by NY 30, and numerous roadside areas in the lake's northeast arm.

Stream Fishing

Many of the streams entering Great Sacandaga hold fine populations of brook, brown, and rainbow trout. You might consider Hans, Kenyetto, and Sand creeks, to name a few. These and other streams, including the Sacandaga River, are generously stocked with trout by the New York State Department of Environmental Conservation (DEC) and are generally lightly fished for much of the season. Because of the nature of the terrain in the

Twenty pounds of Great Sacandaga northern. Fish twice this size may yet lurk in the lake where Peter Dubuc once took a world-record pike.

Great Sacandaga area, streams can range from slow-moving, sand-bottomed watercourses to typical boulder-strewn mountain streams with numerous pools and riffles. Any bait or tackle shop, service station, or general store can direct you to the nearest trout stream and can suggest the best way to fish it. Information available from the DEC and the Fulton and Saratoga County chambers of commerce will also help you pick out the streams you may want to fish.

Peck's Lake

We'll depart the Great Sacandaga Lake region now and head west on NY 30A and NY 29A in search of other piscatorial adventures. A half-hour drive from Great Sacandaga brings us to Peck's Lake on NY 29A. This is an eminently fishable, privately owned body of water that holds excellent populations of northern, largemouth, smallmouth, pickerel, walleye, and an abundance of panfish, and it has consistently produced prizewinning fish. This 1,400-acre lake has a maximum depth of about 40 feet and features the type of rocky, stump-filled structure that seems to spell "fish." Launch facilities, camping, cottages, bait, and boat and motor rentals are available at the lake. Rates and additional information can be obtained by writing to Peck's Lake Fishing Resort (NY 29A, Gloversville, NY 12078).

The Caroga Lakes

A few miles north, near the intersection of NY 10 and NY 29A, we encounter East and West Caroga lakes, both top-notch fishing waters. They offer a mixed bag of everything from bass and splake to smelt, pickerel, and panfish. Walleyes have also been stocked here and offer additional sport. The lakes are also popular ice-fishing destinations. The shorelines are pretty well filled by summer homes and camps, but fishing access is still available. There's a popular state-operated campsite on East Caroga, off NY 29A, and launch facilities are also offered. Boat passage between the two lakes is made easy by a small connecting channel.

Canada Lake

A stone's throw away, on NY 10/29A, is Canada Lake. The 525-acre lake has a maximum depth of 144 feet and holds lake trout, which are stocked annually by the DEC. Pickerel, smallmouth, and panfish are also present in generous numbers. There are commercial boat liveries on the lake as well as a state-operated launch site. Pine Lake, a few miles north of Canada Lake, also offers good pickerel, bass, and panfish angling.

Nine Corner Lake

Let's now do some walk-in fishing. Nine Corner Lake lies just west of Pine Lake and is easily reached by a gentle trail less than a mile long. The well-marked trailhead is located on NY 29A, a few hundred feet beyond where NY 29A and NY 10 part company. Nine Corner had suffered a bit in the past from acid rain, but liming helped, and it receives generous annual infusions of brook trout. Shore-fishing access on this body of water is excellent, although a canoe, float tube, or inflatable craft will help you cover more of the bays that give it its name. If conditions are right, you may even get a look at the resident loons. Fish this water as you would any north country pond, but I again recommend a Lake Clear Wabbler with a worm-baited trailer hook. It works as well on trout as it does on Great Sacandaga's walleyes. If fishing from shore, try small Mepps spinners, Phoebes, and similar lures, though fly tossers will also find this lake productive.

Stream Fishing

We are now traveling west on NY 29A. Various trailheads along the way lead the angler to other, more remote fishing waters. If stream fishing is your preference, you may want to consider any of a dozen or more streams that course through this area and harbor scrappy browns, brookies, or rainbows. Those that are stocked annually by the DEC include Caroga, Mayfield, McQueen, and Zimmerman creeks, to name just a few. A good topographic or county map will help you locate these creeks as well as others that are not stocked but hold native populations of trout. The DEC also publishes annual stocking reports, which can help you track down waters you may want to fish.

The next port of call in our westward trek along NY 29A and NY 29 is East Canada Creek. Flowing south out of the 147,454-acre Ferris Wild Forest, East Canada offers fine fishing for brookies and browns. It's a clear, cold-water stream that features deep holes, tempting riffles, and stretches that beckon to the fly fisherman. East Canada is good fishing water throughout the trout season, even during the warmer months. As we traverse

NY 29A and then hook up with NY 29, bear in mind that the area to the north is as wildly beautiful and remote as areas found deeper in the Adirondacks. Fishing opportunities abound and are much too numerous to mention here, but this is where homework is important. Again, a good topographic map, some imagination, and all the information you can gather will open up dozens of new and exciting fishing opportunities.

Hinckley Reservoir

At Middleville, NY 29 hooks up with NY 28. Follow this road up to NY 365, and you're in the extreme northwest corner of our area. Here you'll find Hinckley Reservoir. With some 24 miles of shoreline, a picnic area, a boat launch, and a recreation area, it offers an excellent north country angling and camping opportunity. Hinckley is another of those mixed-bag waters with something for everyone—pickerel, some trout, bass, panfish, and more.

West Canada Creek

Let's backtrack now. That beautiful, tempting stream you were crossing and paralleling as you traveled northward on NY 28 was West Canada Creek, once rated in the top five of New York State's top 50 trout streams. To our Native Americans it was called Canata—stream of amber water. Though primarily brown trout water, sizable brookies are also available in the upper stretches of this 26-mile-long fishery. West Canada is popular and productive throughout the season, attracting trout fans of every ilk—waders, bank walkers, and canoeists. It supports a healthy native population of trout, generously complemented by some thirty thousand hatchery-bred brethren stocked annually along its length. During the summer months it produces some good-sized bass in certain areas, but big trout are what you're here for. West Canada features big, deep, slow-moving stretches as well as faster water, offering every angler the opportunity to pursue his or her favorite method of angling. For most, however, this is prime fly-fishing water, and all I can suggest by way of patterns is to "match the hatch." Mayfly, nymph, black gnat, Coachman—you name it, it will produce as on any other trout water at the appropriate time and place. Your favorite spinner or small crankbait will also work well. Bait fishermen will find that live minnows or worms drifted near the bottom will consistently produce trout. However, there are no-kill and artificials-only stretches along the West Canada, so be sure to check your creek map and local regulations carefully, though these special areas are generally well marked.

In the early spring, West Canada runs high, fast, and cold, and this will dictate your fishing methods more than any other factor. The area below the dam at Trenton Falls is subject to sudden water releases from the power generating plant located there. There are no set schedules for these releases, and the wading angler should be constantly on the alert for signs of rapidly rising water. This is especially important in the trophy section below the falls, which begins at Trenton Falls Bridge and extends about 2½ miles downstream to the mouth of Cincinnati Creek. The creel limit is three, minimum size 12 inches, and artificial lures only are allowed. NY 28 parallels West Canada for much of its length, and roadside access is readily available for miles of excellent trout fishing.

Continuing south on NY 28, you can hook up with NY 29 at Middleville and head east through the southern reaches of our designated area. You're probably tired of fishing by now, but there's plenty left as we head back along NY 29 to NY 30 and our starting point. As you're heading back east along NY 29, plan on fishing Spruce Creek in the township of Salisbury. It's great water and harbors some fine brown trout. Spruce enters the East Canada at Dolgeville, and you'll be paralleling the creek for a while before entering the village. Other good trout waters on your route back include Middle Sprite and Meco creeks.

We've completed our cook's tour through waters inhabited by largemouth and smallmouth bass, northern, trout, walleye, bullhead, splake, pickerel, and every imaginable species of native New York State panfish—all a stone's throw from wilderness to the north and the Mohawk Valley immediately to our south. Staying on the roads plotted in this chapter will keep you within 25 miles of the New York State Thruway most of the time, but the angling opportunities you'll encounter are more than you could do justice to in a dozen seasons.

For more information, write to the following local organizations:
• Fulton County Chamber of Commerce, 2 N. Main St., Gloversville, NY 12078
• Great Sacandaga Lake Association, Box 900, Northville, NY 12134
• Great Sacandaga Lake Fisheries Federation, P.O. Box 991, Northville, NY 12134
• Peck's Lake Fishing Resort, NY 29A, Gloversville, NY 12078

About the Author

Ron Kolodziej is an ardent fisherman and hunter who lives in Amsterdam, New York, and has fished extensively "just north of the Thruway." He was a licensed fishing guide on Great Sacandaga Lake for over two decades. An outdoor columnist for the *Amsterdam Recorder* for more than 37 years, he has also written for *New York Game & Fish*, *NYS Conservationist* magazine, *Upland Fishing*, and southern Adirondack area newspapers. He is a nationally acclaimed, award-winning writer and an active member of many outdoor groups, including the New York State Outdoor Writers Association (past president), the Outdoor Writers Association of America, the Professional Outdoor Media Association, the New England Outdoor Writers Association, and the Great Sacandaga Lake Fisheries Federation, as well as an inductee in the NYS Outdoorsmen Hall of Fame.

CHAPTER THIRTEEN

The Great Southwestern Wilderness

Don Williams

W hat is the most remote area in northern New York? This is a common question for both backpackers and anglers. Certainly, the Cold River area west of Mount Marcy is very remote. So is the interior portion of Tug Hill. And the upper Oswegatchie is very far from anything.

But perhaps the largest wild area of the Adirondacks is what we will call the great southwestern wilderness.

Nine topographic quadrangles define this region: Raquette Lake, Big Moose, Number Four, McKeever, Old Forge, West Canada Lakes, Piseco Lake, Ohio, and Remsen. This vast area encompasses some 1.3 million acres, much of it public or state land. NY 28 runs through the upper portion of this area, and NY 8 slices through the lower part. Both highways intersect with NY 30 (the Adirondack Trail) on the east and NY 12 on the west.

The southwestern Adirondacks abound with state land, some of it designated wilderness and some wild forest. Unit management plans have been

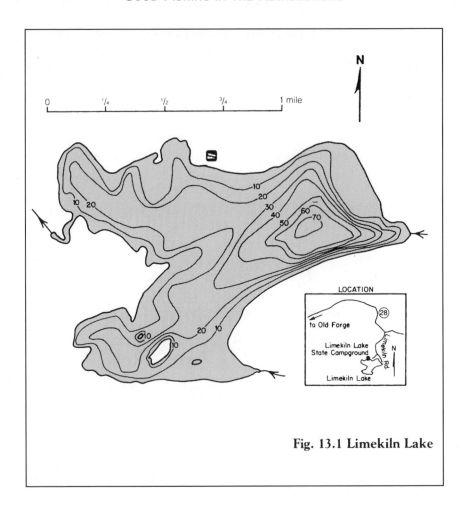

Fig. 13.1 Limekiln Lake

developed by the Adirondack Park Agency and the Department of Environmental Conservation (DEC), and these define the usage of this part of the Adirondack Forest Preserve. The Ha-De-Ron-Dah Wilderness Area, West Canada Lake Wilderness, Moose River Plains Wild Forest, and Black River Wild Forest, along with Ferris Lake Wild Forest and portions of Pigeon Lake Wilderness, are all found within the great southwestern tract. In this unspoiled setting you can hunt, hike, ski, canoe, and fish. In the wilderness areas, there will be neither sounds nor sights of civilization. In the wild forest areas, some motorized use may be permitted. Old wood roads and trails open up the remote fishing ponds and streams to the avid angler. State campgrounds include Alger Island, Brown Tract Pond, Fourth and Eighth lakes,

Golden Beach, Limekiln Lake, Hinckley Reservoir, Nicks Lake, Little Sand Point, Point Comfort, and Poplar Beach.

This region has spawned fish stories for a long time. In fact, stories of great catches have been circulating since the 1840 Lake Piseco Trout Club reports in the American edition of Izaak Walton's *Compleat Angler*. Those who read the book remember the 2 tons of trout taken from Piseco Lake in a five-year period.

Piseco Lake

Piseco Lake continues to bring good fishing to anglers today. It is especially noted for its good ice fishing. Lying close to NY 8 adjacent to Piseco village, it is easily reached over well-plowed winter roads by a drive through the village to the back side of the lake. About 2½ miles from the NY 8 turn to Piseco, you will spot the fishing shanties. In any event, stop before you get to the Poplar Point State Campground. The best fishing is off that point. Adirondack ice fishing can be very cold, but it can also be beautiful. A sunny winter afternoon on a snow-covered Adirondack lake, surrounded by mountain walls and good company, is truly an uplifting experience. Add to this image a 22-inch lake trout coming up through the ice, and the picture is complete.

Piseco Lake is stocked with lake trout yearly. One of the recent stocking lists included 8,700 6-inch lake trout. A winter catch may include a mixture of stocked and native trout. The natives are darker, with some white at the edges of the pectoral and ventral fins. Stocked fish tend to have a more silvery color. Colors aside, lake trout is one of the most delectable of the trout family.

Anglers who find Piseco Lake to be one of the best winter fishing lakes around know how to get those lakers. They follow the traditional ice-fishing methods: tip-ups baited with minnows securely fastened in the back with small treble hooks. The springing up of a tip-up triggers the angler's adrenaline, but a quick rush and a fast pull will lose the fish. The trick is to move slowly, let the hook set, and play the fish a while. Caution pays off when a yellow-dotted laker is gently pulled through the open fish hole.

Piseco Lake is also a popular fishing lake during the warmer months. Good smallmouth bass fishing can be found in the north end of the lake. Stay near the middle and the west side; it is rocky near the island. Fishing off the weedy areas has also produced some bass for the summer angler. Whitefish, bullhead, perch, and pickerel are other species caught during the summer months. There are three state campsites on the lake—Poplar Point, Point Comfort, and Little Sand Point—with boat launching available at all three. Nearby hamlets can supply your needs, and the adjacent mountains, streams, and trails make it a great place to spend a fishing vacation.

West Canada Creek

Another good fishing bet in the southwestern Adirondacks is West Canada Creek. Rising high in the Adirondacks, it is dammed by Hinckley Reservoir, then meanders down to the Mohawk River.

West Canada Creek was once listed in a DEC publication as being near the top of the state's "fishiest 50" trout streams. Good trout fishermen agree. It can be fished successfully from beginning to end. Much of the best fishing is found near the bridges, the old bridge abutments near Poland, angler parking areas below Poland and above Middleville, and the roadside fishing areas between Newport and Middleville. The biggest fish are taken in the spring in the cold mountain waters above Hinckley. Good fish may be found near spring holes during the summer. The lower part of West Canada is discussed further in chapter 12.

The upper reaches of West Canada are remote and are right in the heart of the southwestern wilderness. State land surrounds the South Branch, which flows roughly east to west and joins the main river at Nobleboro. The main branch goes northeast up through the town of Morehouse to West Canada Lakes. Most of the main branch is surrounded by public lands. Fish the spots where feeder streams enter the main branch, and fish up into some of the feeder streams. The riffle sections are usually productive. Minnows and worms work best in the deep pools during the early spring; flies, spinners, spoons, small plugs, and worms work as the water warms. The most popular fly seems to be the Royal Coachman. Phoebes and Mepps are popular spinning lures.

Limekiln Lake

Now move on to try your luck in Limekiln Lake. It can be reached by taking NY 28 east from Utica or NY 28 west from Blue Mountain Lake. Limekiln Lake is the western gateway for the Moose River Recreation Area. The entrance is reached by following a road running south and just east of the hamlet of Inlet.

The Great Southwestern Wilderness is for backpackers and boaters alike. Parts of this area are very remote and offer excellent trout-fishing opportunities in a wild setting.

Limekiln Lake is one of the cleanest bodies of water in the state. It is rated "A"—safe to drink—although all water should be purified before drinking. The 460-acre lake also holds an "A" trout rating. The number of fish a lake supports is stated in pounds per surface area, and at 100 pounds per surface acre we find that Limekiln Lake holds a good supply of fish. Limekiln Lake Campground offers a boat launch, so all of the angler's needs are satisfied: a good lake, a supply of fish, nearby bait and tackle stores, a campground, and a launching site.

Splake have been stocked in Limekiln Lake for many years. Those who like brook trout and lake trout will love splake fishing, because a splake is a cross between the two. The state record is 13.8 pounds, caught in Limekiln Lake in 2004. Regular catches range from 2 to 8 pounds. The cove areas of Limekiln supply some of the best summer fishing.

The Moose River Plains

Leaving Limekiln Lake, we move into the Moose River Plains area, one of the wildest sections of the Adirondacks. Mostly state land, it abounds with fine fishing streams and ponds. The South Branch of the Moose River runs somewhat parallel to the southern side of the Moose River access road, and the road crosses several feeder streams. Other streams and ponds in the area can be reached via an extensive trail system. Secondary roads and old log roads also run through the area, providing additional access.

You may want to check the up-to-date regulations for the Moose River Recreation Area by getting the latest brochure from the DEC. No outboard motors are allowed, nor is the use of live baitfish. Other restrictions may also apply.

The Moose River was also listed in the "fishiest 50." Besides the 30-mile-long South Branch of the Moose River, there is also the North Branch, which flows out of big Moose Lake near Eagle Bay, and the Middle Branch, near Old Forge. Depending on where you fish, you may encounter brook, brown, or rainbow trout. All sections have brook trout, and the other species can be found from McKeever west. Once you are in the Moose River Plains, good fishing can be found almost anywhere. It is not unusual to catch a limit in the main stream or by fishing up one of the feeder streams. You may take any size trout during the season, with the daily limit being 10.

Cedar River Flow

The Cedar River Flow is the place to go if you own a small craft such as a pram, guide boat, or canoe. It is a picturesque place to while away your fishing hours, and it is well stocked with brook trout.

The Cedar River Flow is the eastern gateway to the Moose River Wilderness. It is best reached by driving to Indian Lake on NY 30 and continuing through the village, crossing the Cedar River bridge, and turning left at the next corner. You will see a cemetery on the left just before the turn. Proceed down the Cedar River Road until you reach the end. You will find the flow right at the entrance to the recreation area.

The Cedar River Flow is a great place to see trout feeding on flies and to try your luck at outsmarting them with some fly-casting. Worms also work, though according to Izaak Walton, "Our hands have long been washed from the dirty things, satisfied not to fish when the fly cannot be used"! If you don't subscribe to this, know that mountain trout also love grasshoppers and crickets. If all else fails, try a kernel of corn or a piece of tomato. They work!

The time of day is important in fishing these Adirondack waters. During the early spring and late fall, the trout feed during the middle of the day, especially when it is sunny. In the warm weather, trout are generally feeding during the morning and evening. In any case, watch closely for signs of surface feeding, and you will multiply your chances for a successful catch. Fish the shores around the weeds when the Adirondack bugs are bouncing on the surface of the water.

For fishing such a large, remote area, you may want to give some thought to hiring a good fishing guide. Competent and reliable guides are available to make your trip safe and successful. Once the guide has shown you the fishing secrets of the Cedar River Flow, the West Canada Wilderness, or the Moose River Plains, you can choose to go with or without a guide on your future trips.

The Fulton Chain of Lakes

The Fulton Chain of Lakes on NY 28 has long been popular for fishing. First Lake can be found sprawling east from the village of Old Forge, 50 miles northeast of Utica. The eight lakes stretch northeast for some 15 miles from that point almost to Raquette Lake. They can be seen and are easily reached from main highways. First, Second, and Third lakes are closely connected by small passages. A longer, winding passage leads to the largest lake on the Fulton Chain, Fourth Lake. The hamlet of Inlet is at the head of Fourth Lake. Fifth Lake is a small pond not connected by passable waters to Sixth Lake. Seventh and Eighth lakes are sizable lakes and, along with Fourth Lake, are popular fishing spots.

Fourth Lake is a good choice for a variety of fishing opportunities. Lake trout are taken in the spring along the shores, and from the middle of June through the summer they are taken from the deeper waters. The deeper areas out from Eagle Bay and south of Cedar Island are good spots for trolling. Start the season with silver Rapalas, and use some of your better "action" spoons later on.

Landlocked salmon, an introduced species, can be taken during the same periods. In the early season they are in the shallower areas, especially where the feeder streams come in. Minnow-imitating lures and flies are used.

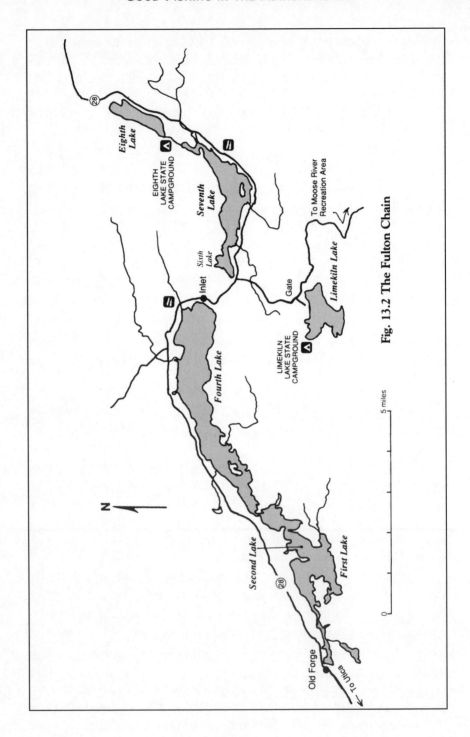

Fig. 13.2 The Fulton Chain

Trolling throughout the summer pays off. Try trolling near the surface during the early morning in the roughly triangular area formed by Cedar Island, Dollar Island, and Inlet. A New York State boat launch is located at Inlet right on NY 28. A marina and boat launch can also be found in Inlet, and a state launch site/picnic area is available at the end of Fourth Lake on South Shore Road.

Those who like shore fishing will find Fourth Lake a good bet during May. A big attraction is the rainbows, which can be taken by casting from shore with live bait. A section near NY 28 just east of Barton Island holds good promise. Shore fishing can be practiced throughout the summer, although trolling is the preferred method then. Add some Christmas Trees to your usual lures to attract the rainbows. The best spots are always near the islands.

Smallmouth bass are also present in Fourth Lake, with the best concentrations usually being found at the east end of the lake and in the small bays along the south shore. Evening fishing pays off when pursuing the smallmouths here. Popular lures such as Hula Poppers, Rapalas, and Mepps are put to work, and crabs (crawfish) and minnows are employed throughout the season.

Brown and brook trout are found at the west end of Fourth Lake near Alger Island. Spin-casting with lures, fishing with live bait, and trolling with small plugs and spoons can all help to put a few browns and brookies in the frying pan.

Seventh Lake also has a convenient boat launch site on NY 28. The lake and the launch site are well marked and easily located. Seventh Lake provides much the same fishing as Fourth Lake, but it is not as large. New York State stocks Seventh Lake with rainbows, lakers, splake, and landlocked salmon. It is one of the best waters for splake fishing. Sixth Lake is also stocked with brook trout.

Eighth Lake is as popular as Fourth Lake in the Fulton Chain. The Eighth Lake campsite, 5 miles west of Raquette Lake village, provides access and a place to stay. Eighth Lake is stocked with rainbows, lakers, and landlocked salmon. Anglers come from miles around to get those rainbows during the summer months. Getting an early start pays off, and the best fishing spot is near the island in the east end. Trolling the section toward the highway with a Christmas Tree rig often attracts the rainbows that call Eighth Lake home.

Remote Ponds

One of the greatest outdoor experiences is to backpack and bushwhack into a remote pond for fishing. It is worth the effort whether you choose to rely on your own outdoor skills or play it safe with a guide. Backpack angling moves fishing one step further from the norm and provides a challenge for those with the gumption to try it.

There are 174 ponds in the southwestern Adirondack area, and 88 of them hold a trout (T) designation. Study a topographic map and pick the one that looks best to you. The list includes three Beaver Ponds, six Buck Ponds, three Deer Ponds, four East Ponds, three Grass Ponds, six Mud Ponds, three Rock Ponds, and three Round Ponds—all rated for fish survival and/or trout. Some of the stocked ponds that you may see on the maps are Bear Pond, Bullhead Pond, Clear Pond, and Twin Pond. The complete list is available from the DEC each year. Just pick a pond and make your plans.

Planning a Trip

How do we do it? We select the area we want to fish from a topographic map. For illustration, let's pick the Old Forge Quadrangle. This quadrangle is number G210 on the key to New York State topographic maps. This number is important, in case the pond we pick is one of those several mentioned that share the same name. Fishing in the wrong pond could be an unsuccessful venture.

We may want to vacation and fish near the Fulton Chain of Lakes and also have access to the South Branch of the Moose River. We will make our base camp near Old Forge and locate a pond in that area for our fishing hike.

Bisby Road runs south out of Old Forge village to the Bisby Chain of Lakes (another fishing possibility). Almost 3 miles out of the village, the road crosses a trail that leads to Rock Pond at about the same spot it crosses the outlet of Little Moose Lake. Rock Pond is one of five waters by that name in the southwest Adirondacks. However, the one in this quadrangle is rated high for trout fishing.

The hike in to Rock Pond would take less than an hour, and for those interested, another short hike would take them to some fishing on the South Branch of the Moose River. Those motivated for an extended backpacking trip could spend several days in this area trying out the fishing waters.

Other ponds can be found the same way. Another example might be a look at a reclaimed trout pond such as Jakes Pond in the Number Four quadrangle. Some ponds are more remote than these, but the fish are there for those who want to go after them. No one can guarantee a successful trip, but your chances are multiplied when you get into the less-fished waters of the southwest Adirondacks.

About the Author

Don Williams is an Adirondack guide and a retired school administrator from Gloversville.

Winter dies hard on Tug Hill. Often, deep snowbanks will greet
you on April excursions to the rich trout waters of the Hill.

CHAPTER FOURTEEN

The Secret Streams of Tug Hill

Allen Benas

T ug Hill is a large, elevated land mass located in the northern New York State counties of Lewis, Jefferson, Oneida, and Oswego. While largely ignored by outside anglers, its 1.2 million acres offer some of the best wilderness trout fishing opportunities in the state.

Although Tug Hill is little more than an hour's drive from Utica, Syracuse, and Watertown, it is time spent traveling back in history—back to the days when people were few, and the quiet remoteness of the surroundings made you wonder if anyone had ever stepped foot exactly where you were standing at the moment. This vast area, its silence interrupted only by the sounds of nature, is inspiring.

Today, Tug Hill is best known for receiving the greatest amount of snowfall east of the Rockies. Its average annual snowfall of 260 inches (with a record of 355 inches) makes it a major source of water for the Black and Mohawk-Hudson River systems. Recreationally, this snowfall makes the Hill one of the most popular cross-country skiing and snowmobiling areas in northern New York.

The area experienced its greatest population growth during the mid- to

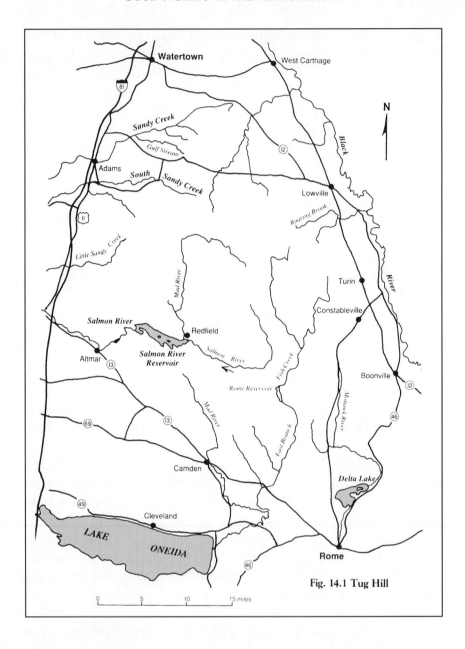

Fig. 14.1 Tug Hill

late 1800s. Because it was a prime timber area, towns grew, new timber camps sprang up, and the railroad expanded its service area to haul the tons of spruce, hemlock, and pine needed by the growing cities that surrounded it. The timber industry prospered until the early 1900s.

Agriculture followed the timber industry. However, farmers faced with the combination of short growing seasons and extreme amounts of precipitation found their efforts exhausting and often futile. The majority of farms were deserted by the 1940s, and the land quickly reverted to a wilderness character. The demands put forth by nature created a bond among those who stayed on the Hill, as it did their fellow frontiersmen who had moved west decades before. Those who live on the Hill today have retained this feeling of togetherness and seem eager to extend their hands in friendship to those desirous of making the Hill a part of their lives.

Fishing in Tug Hill

Tug Hill trout streams reflect the region and range—from small wild brook trout streams to larger streams (such as the East and West branches of Fish Creek, which support populations of wild and stocked brown trout as well as wild brook trout) to the lower Salmon River (with large runs of steelhead, chinook, and coho salmon). With this diversity of angling opportunity, coupled with an array of streams too numerous to list, Tug Hill offers the trout hunter some fine fishing in a remote, uncrowded setting.

The headwaters of the Deer River, along with North and South Sandy creeks, are located on the northern portion of Tug Hill in Jefferson and Lewis counties. These streams are well known to local anglers for their excellent wild brook trout fishing, particularly during May and early June. The majority of fish are in the 7- to 10-inch range, but brookies up to 15 inches are not uncommon. The best baits are worms or small spinners. Spinners are most effective when cast upstream and retrieved downstream slightly faster than the current. Some of the best streams are Raystone, Abijah, and the upper reaches of South Sandy Creek in the vicinity of Worth Center. South of the hamlet of Barnes Corners are the East and West branches of the Deer River, the upper reaches of the Mad River, Edick Creek, and Sears Pond. Also, North Sandy Creek above the village of Adams is stocked with brown trout, and each spring holdover trout in the 15- to 17-inch range are caught. These streams are generally small and brushy, and best fished with short fishing rods and hip boots. Because the best fishing coincides with the peak of the blackfly season, a good supply of insect repellent is recommended.

The Salmon River watershed is located on the western slope of Tug Hill, primarily in Lewis and Oswego counties. It flows westerly through Pulaski and enters Lake Ontario at Port Ontario. Above Redfield Reservoir, the East

Branch of the Salmon is a high-quality wild brown and brook trout stream. The brook trout generally range up to 12 inches and are abundant. Brown trout are found in the deeper pools, and DEC electrofishing surveys indicate that fish in the 15- to 20-inch range are common. However, the browns are difficult to catch, and best success is achieved by fishing early mornings or late evenings with large streamers or live bait.

These upper reaches of the Salmon River range from 20 to 50 feet wide, with pools in excess of 4 feet deep and a bottom of clean gravel. The water is gin clear, and a careful approach improves fishing success. Summer dry-fly fishing is at times outstanding.

The state has acquired more than 20 miles of public fishing rights on the upper Salmon and its tributaries. Tributaries with public fishing rights that provide wild brook trout fishing are the lower Mad River, North Branch Salmon River, and Fall, Mallory, Stony, and Prince brooks. These streams are similar to those found on the north slope of Tug Hill, and the same fishing techniques will prove effective.

Below Redfield Reservoir, the Salmon River supports the largest salmon and steelhead runs in the Lake Ontario drainage basin, providing year-round angling opportunities. Salmon in the 30-plus-pound range and steelhead more than 10 pounds are common. Effective techniques and angling locations vary with the seasons and timing of the runs. Current information can be obtained by calling the Oswego County Fishing Hotline (315-342-5873) or by contacting one of the numerous tackle shops in Pulaski. DEC's Salmon River fish hatchery is located on the river at Altmar and is open to the public daily. The hatchery raises steelhead, chinook, and coho salmon.

Between Lowville and Boonville in Lewis County, a number of streams flow down the east slope of the Hill into the Black River. The character of these streams is markedly different from those just discussed. They have steeper gradients, small waterfalls and gorges, bedrock and broken rubble streambeds, and more variable seasonal flows. The upper reaches of these streams provide fishing for wild brook trout, while the lower portions are generally stocked with brook and brown trout. Wild browns are also present in a number of streams. Good fishing can be found throughout the season in Roaring Brook, Whetstone Creek, Douglas Creek, Mill Creek (Turin), House Creek, the Sugar River and tributaries, and Mill Creek (Boonville).

These streams have generally good access and can be fished effectively with spinning and fly tackle. Fishing pressure is low, and it is not unusual to catch trout in the 12- to 15-inch range. Whetstone Marsh Pond near the village of Martinsburg is stocked with tiger muskellunge and provides the unique opportunity to catch this hybrid of the muskellunge and northern pike. Tigers to 12 pounds are not uncommon here.

Fish Creek

Undoubtedly the best trout fishing on Tug Hill is found on its south slope in the East and West branches of Fish Creek, located in southern Lewis and northern Oneida counties. The Fish Creek watershed is large, and both branches have numerous large and small tributaries. There are many road crossings. The DEC has acquired approximately 55 miles of public fishing rights on the East Branch and its tributaries and 28 miles on the West Branch system. In spite of the high fishing quality and excellent angler access, fishing pressure is generally light.

The Oneida County section of the East Branch from the village of Taberg upstream to Rome Reservoir is big water with fast runs and deep pools. Along with a wild brown and brook trout population, portions of the stream are stocked with yearling brown trout. The East Branch provides excellent fly-fishing water. Large stone fly nymphs fished in the deeper runs in the early morning are particularly effective. Dry-fly fishing is also good, and there is usually a good green drake hatch in early June. This section is open to fishing until November 1, and spectacular catches can be made with minnows during late October, especially just below Rome Reservoir. Rome Reservoir itself is stocked with brown trout, and fish up to 4 pounds are fairly common. Fishing is difficult because of the large minnow population in the reservoir.

Fishing pressure in the Lewis County section of the East Branch above Rome Reservoir is light, although fishing quality is excellent. The stream provides good fly-, spin-, and bait-fishing opportunities. A favorite section locally is off the Stinebricker Road in the town of Lewis. The East Branch has many excellent tributaries. Generally, all the smaller ones support populations of wild brook or brown trout. Some of the larger tributaries that provide good fishing are Furnace, Florence, Fall, Point Rock, and Alder creeks. Besides wild trout, the lower reaches of each are stocked annually.

In contrast to the East Branch, the West Branch is generally a slow meandering stream, particularly above the village of Camden in Oneida County. It is floatable from the Westdale Dam in Oswego County downstream to Camden. The section is hard to fish but can provide the determined angler with browns in the 2- to 4-pound range. Live-bait fishing is the most productive technique. Below Camden, the stream is similar to the East Branch, providing good fly- and spin-fishing for brown trout. Particularly good fishing can be found in the following tributaries: Little River, Mad River, Thompson Creek, and Walker Brook.

At the confluence of the two branches at Blossvale, Fish Creek begins the transition from a cold- to cool-water stream. Smallmouth bass and walleye become more frequent, but large brown trout in the 4- to 6-pound range are regularly taken on live bait. A particularly productive area is off Passer Road in the town of Verona.

Three other overlooked streams originate on the south slope of the Hill. They are the East and West branches of the Mohawk River and the Lansingkill in the towns of Boonville, Ava, and Western in Oneida County. All three provide excellent fishing for wild and stocked brown and brook trout. The Lansingkill in the gorge between Boonville and Westernville is particularly good. Both branches of the Mohawk have relatively long, tough-to-reach sections that provide excellent fly-fishing for brown trout in the 10- to 14-inch range for those willing to walk.

Planning Your Trip

By now it should be apparent that county highway maps or appropriate United States Geological Survey (USGS) quadrangle maps are essential to finding the various streams and locations discussed. Highway maps can be purchased from the appropriate county clerk's office for a nominal fee. The *DeLorme New York Atlas and Gazetteer* is an excellent source for a compendium of topo maps for the entire state.

The ambience of the Hill is not a state of mind but very real. It offers an opportunity to relive what many consider the golden days, when it was people against the elements throughout the year, and survival during the harsh winters was a daily chore. In truth, the type of experience that some anglers travel the world in search of can be enjoyed right here in this region of New York.

More in-depth information on Tug Hill is available from the Temporary State Commission on Tug Hill and the New York State Department of Environmental Conservation, both at the NYS Office Building, 317 Washington Street, Watertown, NY 13601.

About the Author

Allen Benas is a widely experienced St. Lawrence River fishing guide and resort owner. He writes actively about the outdoors and is a member of the Outdoor Writers Association of America. Besides the St. Lawrence, he has fished and hunted farther afield, with the trout streams of Tug Hill being one of the places he dotes on.

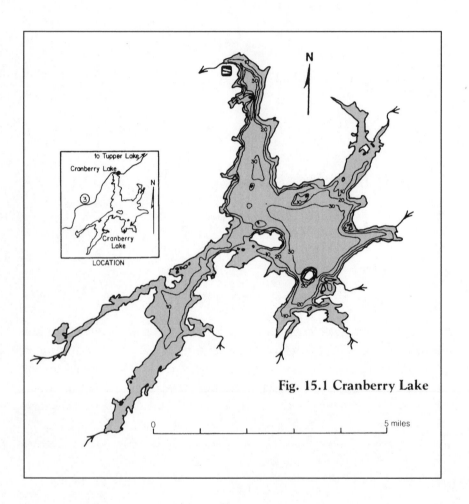

Fig. 15.1 Cranberry Lake

CHAPTER FIFTEEN

Back in Time on the Oswegatchie

Peter O'Shea

One of the most cherished adventures of early-20th-century sportsmen—a canoe trek up the legendary Oswegatchie Inlet of Cranberry Lake in pursuit of its fabled brook trout—can still be experienced by modern anglers. The truly large brookies that once tempted the nation's fishermen and famed naturalists like Ernest Thompson Seton for the most part no longer exist. Much remains, though, not the least of which is the wilderness aura, one that increases as the distance from the launching site lengthens. Amid the beautiful surroundings, one can still thrill to the pursuit of the smaller trout that are present today, both in the Oswegatchie itself and in Cranberry Lake, the body of water it feeds.

Cranberry Lake

Cranberry Lake itself, now approximately 11 square miles in extent, doubled in size with the erection of a dam more than a century ago. The dam flooded not only part of the Oswegatchie but also many of the lake's small feeder streams. These flooded inlets, or flows, were once the place to fish for the lunker trout. The flooding also created a rather circular main body of water open to the west winds and a series of shallow, sheltered inlets spiraling away like the spokes of a wheel.

The inadvertent introduction of yellow perch around 1945 led to the rapid demise of the renowned brook trout fishery. Smallmouth bass were introduced about 1960, and a fairly successful fishery for this species was established shortly thereafter. However, in the late 1970s, acid rain begin to lower the pH of the lake, and this led to a sharp reduction in the number of yellow perch. With the decline of this competing species, brook trout became reestablished in Cranberry Lake starting about 1980. The lake is now stocked regularly with brook trout, and, in addition, there is some natural reproduction over the gravel beds of the river inlet in autumn. There still remains some fair fishing for smallmouth bass on occasion. Deep casting in the flows can be effective, especially in late July or August. Fishing the deeper waters off some of the lake's many islands can also prove rewarding at this time. Sears Island is one that comes to mind; try using live crayfish here.

Early in the year and during September, carefully fishing the shoals off the various flows will prove most productive. These shoal areas are marked by buoys in some cases.

Both Rapalas of different colors and live minnows have proven effective on smallmouth bass through the years on Cranberry. Rock bass weighing as much as ½ pound are also present here, particularly in the flows. They are susceptible to worms and various small spinners. Dead Creek Flow is a good bet for both rock bass and the occasional lunker smallmouth bass. Smallmouth weighing as much as 6 pounds have been taken. Brook trout fishing in the main lake is often best in the flows, particularly just after ice-out in early spring. The Cucumber Hole, one of the many bays of Dead Creek Flow, often proves rewarding for brook trout fanciers at this time.

Cranberry Lake is reached by proceeding west on NY 3 for 26 miles from the village of Tupper Lake to the hamlet of Cranberry Lake. Both food and lodging are available in the hamlet. A Department of Environmental Conservation (DEC) campground is located just outside the village; turn south off NY 3 onto Lone Pine Road and go about ⅓ mile to the campground entrance. It is usually open from Memorial Day through October. A bait and tackle shop is also located in the village.

Approximately 80 percent of the shoreline of Cranberry Lake is forest preserve, as are a number of the many islands that dot the lake, including Joe Indian (the largest). Designated sites have been assigned for primitive camping here by the DEC. Boats may be launched from the DEC boat launching site located in the village on Columbian Road just south of NY 3.

The Famous Oswegatchie

The main feeder of Cranberry Lake is the Oswegatchie River. It flows approximately 26 miles through the boreal woodlands of the forest preserve, from its source springs in a remote area south of High Falls to its mergence with the lake 2 miles below the hamlet of Wanakena. Except for a few short rapids in low water and one carry around a waterfall, the river is canoeable for 22 miles upstream from a public boat launching site at an uninhabited place on the river called Inlet (see the accompanying map, Fig. 15.2).

Inlet, once the site of a sportsmen's hotel, is reached by turning south on a gravel road approximately 1 mile east of the village of Star Lake and heading south 3 miles through the forest preserve until the road terminates at a grassy parking area adjacent to a bend of the river. The 2 miles of the river below Inlet down to the hamlet of Wanakena are not canoeable but are stocked by the DEC with brook trout. These miles can be fished successfully from the bank, especially where the river forms a pool. Fly-fishing can be rewarding when the various mayfly hatches are swarming, which is often just before dark. The Royal Coachman is one dry fly frequently used here, and the Mickey Finn is a popular streamer pattern. Brown trout, too, are present in this 2-mile stretch of river. In addition to offering exciting fly-fishing opportunities, browns can also be fished with live minnows and with Rooster Tails, lures that seem to be especially favored locally. The red and white Dardevle is another lure that takes many brown trout here.

The Oswegatchie below Cranberry Lake

Before we talk about the most important part of the Oswegatchie, that section upstream of Inlet, a few words should be said about the river below Cranberry Lake.

Below the Cranberry Lake dam, the Oswegatchie flows through 8 miles of a timber company tract that is leased to a sportsmen's club. An industrial dam erected still farther downriver at Newton Falls has widened this stretch so that in most areas it resembles a shallow, marshy lake where nesting loons are present. Brook trout and brown trout are stocked annually here by the DEC and are mostly found just below the dam at Cranberry Lake. Smallmouth bass and northern pike lurk in the wide, shallow areas where the water is warmer. Fishing is not prohibited in this stretch. The chief access is from a sandy ramp diagonally opposite the old Cranberry Lake dump on the Tooley Pond Road, approximately ⅔ mile from its intersection with NY 3.

A canoe can be launched here and paddled for a number of miles downriver with a minimum of encumbrances. As the river meanders and widens, numerous weed beds are seen covering the shallows near the shore. A red and white Dardevle cast from a moving canoe or johnboat can often prove irresistible to northerns; 20-pounders have thrilled anglers here on occasion. The Rebel is another effective lure, and both of these lures can be used to good effect in late September and October as the fishing for northerns improves. Minnows or small yellow perch used in conjunction with a bobber usually bear fruit to varying degrees throughout the year. The smallmouth bass (along with some largemouth) are frequently taken with minnow-imitating lures.

The April 1 opening of the trout season is quite early for this northern clime. On this date, the lake itself is often still ice clad, while the river is still too cold and too high for the successful pursuit of trout. April 20 to May 1 is usually a more realistic time to begin fishing in this area.

The Oswegatchie above Inlet

Fishing the Oswegatchie by canoe is generally productive for brook trout for the whole distance of 22 miles above Inlet. At High Falls, a portage is necessary to gain access to the final 7 miles.

As the canoe glides off from the sandy landing, a sense of tranquility is felt almost immediately. This reflects that the Oswegatchie above Inlet is designated a "wild" river and, as such, motors of any kind are banned. During moderate to high water, the few rapids encountered along the route are navigated fairly easily. At low water, mostly during the summer, a pole can come in handy. You start by paddling upriver against a normally gentle current. However, this current may increase for as much as half a day after heavy rains. The trip downriver usually takes two-thirds the time needed to paddle upstream.

The river meanders slowly, with frequent S-shaped curves giving the paddler ample time to both reflect on the beauty of the surroundings and to cast a worm or lure into the placid waters. (A lure frequently used here is the Panther Martin.) Fishing on the river early in the year can be quite fruitful in

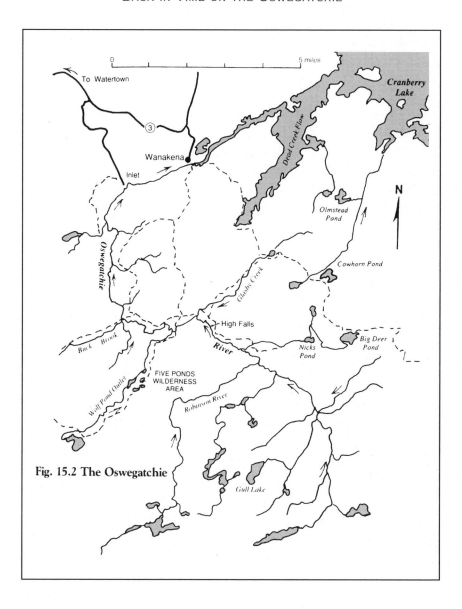

Fig. 15.2 The Oswegatchie

the pools lying at the feet of the several rapids. Heading upriver they are Griffin Rapids, Crooked Rapids, and the pool beneath High Falls. Worms and minnows usually work best at this time of year. The trout taken here, while generally small in size, are delicious and can offer a sporting battle.

During the summer, when the water has warmed up considerably, by far the most productive places to cast a line are around the many "spring holes" encountered along the way. These are areas where a true spring bubbles up from the streambed or, more often, where one of the many tributary streams enters the main river. The water stays cooler here during the summer and is far more attractive to trout during this season. These spring holes or tributaries usually are named and well known locally. Going upriver, you come across them as follows: Otter Creek, Dorsey Creek, High Rock Creek, Cage Lake Spring Hole, Wolf Creek Spring Hole, and Carter's Landing Spring Hole. Worms and small minnows can still produce here even in summer, but spinners and other lures are used with increasing frequency as the summer progresses.

The river ambles on, framed by an almost continuous canopy of balsam fir, tamarack, and white pine. The white pine in a few cases reaches heroic proportions, some trees exceeding 100 feet in height. After a mile, the river enters an open swamp where, amid thick alders, two of the tributary creeks—Otter Creek on the right and Dorsey Creek on the left—add their measure to the Oswegatchie. These are traditional spring holes but will take some searching to discover as their entrances to the river are fairly well obscured.

After a short stretch in which the river straightens out, the Oswegatchie enters into a large boreal wetland for the next several miles. The river now meanders so extremely that local lore has it that an alert paddler can see the back of his neck. At 4½ miles from Inlet, you'll reach High Rock. This is a huge boulder looking over the wide expanse of wetland just passed through. Primitive camping facilities (including a privy) are located at High Rock; a trail leads from here out to the village of Wanakena in 4 miles. Tiny High Rock Creek comes in here also. It is another of the more prominent spring holes along the river. It was near this spot in 1982 that two DEC forest rangers saw a cow moose and her calf swim across the river, the first indication of breeding success for moose to emerge in more than one hundred years in the Adirondacks.

It would be well to mention here that the sights and delights of wildlife add immeasurably to the enjoyment of the entire trip along the river. While there are rivers in the Adirondacks that outstrip the Oswegatchie in the output of trout, few areas surpass it insofar as the quality of wildlife observed and of the wilderness encountered. Therein may lie the ultimate attraction of this small river. Osprey frequently hunt over the river, and often they can be seen plunging in after fish (not trout, we hope!). Loons are often heard, but their calling is from one of the nearby interior ponds—the river itself is too narrow to accommodate them, being only 75 feet at its widest point near

Inlet. Broods of mergansers and black ducks are also commonly seen on the river, while great blue herons hunt for frogs in the shallows all along the river's course.

Beaver are abundant on the river and can often be seen swimming along-side the canoe as dusk approaches. Their dams are not much in evidence as they most often use bank dens along the river, especially below High Falls. Otter are also numerous. They occasionally can be observed sticking their heads above the water like seals, but more often you will notice signs of them in the form of slides and rolling areas in grassy areas on the shore. White-tailed deer are more common here than in many other areas of the Adiron-dacks. They can frequently be seen feeding on the shores, and the stretch of the river from the plains to High Falls is a large winter deer yard. These upper Oswegatchie deer are notable both for their size and the imposing girth of many of their racks. Black bear, too, are quite common along the en-tire length of the river and are occasionally sighted. Much more often bear will make their presence known as they forage for food around the campsite at night. A safety rule when camping along the river is to make sure that all food items are tied high out of the reach of hungry bears and definitely out of the tents.

A short ways upstream from High Rock, the river leaves the wide marsh and enters a long, narrow, relatively straight corridor called the Straight of the Woods. The banks are lined here with the cathedral-like spires of balsam fir until the next prominent spring hole is reached, Griffin Rapids, 6½ miles above Inlet. A DEC lean-to is located here, and the first parcel of unhar-vested or old growth forest is seen on the riverbank. This magnificent stand of sugar maple and beech with an occasional venerable hemlock extends all the way to Buck Pond. The rapids, which are hardly noticeable in medium to high water, provide good fishing (at their heads and also in the pools below) for brook trout of up to 12 inches.

Approximately 8½ miles above Inlet is Cage Lake Spring Hole. A foot-bridge spanning the river and a marked trail going to Buck Pond and Cage Lake previously existed here but were abandoned by the DEC because of the repeated washing out of the bridge in spring floods and to incessant beaver flooding of the hiking trail.

In addition to currently being the site of an excellent spring hole, the area is also the site of another DEC lean-to. As is true at all the lean-tos along the Oswegatchie, there is a noticeable paucity of firewood in the immediate vicinity.

Taking off again, the paddler next comes to an imposing stand of large white pine and tamarack lining the river approximately 12 miles above Inlet. The scenery here is, in many respects, more reminiscent of Alaska than New York State. At 12½ miles the one footbridge still remaining above Inlet is encountered. Crossing the river here is the Five Ponds Trail, which takes you to remote Sand Lake after another 8½ miles of hiking. On the way this trail passes the entrancing Five Ponds themselves, from which the entire Oswegatchie wilderness takes its name. In the vicinity of the five tiny ponds stands a group of magnificent virgin red spruce.

Wolf Creek Outlet is next. This spring hole has produced trout since the days of the early Adirondack guides who had rustic camps in the vicinity. After that, Round Hill Rapids is the next major feature. It and Ross Rapids, a little farther upriver, are two of the more difficult rapids, and in low water a short carry may be necessary. Fishing for brook trout with worms or minnows at the foot of the rapids is productive during early spring. Another mile on, or about 14 miles upstream of Inlet, yet another notable spring hole is reached: Carter Spring Hole. This name refers to the area between Glasby Creek and Moses Rock Spring, an interval of roughly 100 yards. Glasby Creek drains that unique area known as the Plains, a large open area in a region of otherwise uninterrupted forests. The Plains, which covered the valley between Round Top Mountain and Three Mile Mountain, have only recently begun to revert to forest: black cherry, balsam fir, and tamarack. The Plains, however, retain a generally semiopen aspect.

Finally, 15 miles from Inlet, High Falls is reached. At the foot of the rapids extending from the falls is one of the river's traditional fishing hot spots. The falls have been a prime wilderness destination for nearly a century, going back to the era of Dobson's camps, a popular rustic lodge catering to sportsmen. Nestled under handsome white pine and hemlocks, two other DEC lean-tos are located on either side of the river. Several popular, marked hiking trails also converge here.

Immediately above the falls (after a short carry) the river changes character, becoming more narrow with a deeper channel. The trout get smaller but are still present. More of the trout are now of the native strain, distinguished by salmon-colored flesh, and are excellent eating. On occasion, flyfishing can be quite exciting above the falls. Fishing into the current is best, and remember that the main hatches of mayflies and stone flies occur here 10 to 20 days after the hatches in the southern part of New York State. The Black Gnat is one fly to consider using here. At the confluence of the

Oswegatchie and the Robinson rivers, approximately 3 miles above High Falls, good fishing is provided by the food washed into the Oswegatchie by the Robinson. Like the spring holes below the falls, fishing in the pool here remains rewarding throughout the summer. The head of navigation is about 6 or 7 miles above the falls, depending on water levels. It is approximately 3 miles to the junction of the Robinson River, with two notable spring holes between Nick's Pond outlet and Red Horn Creek.

After 2 miles of paddling, you see a ridge with very large pine on the left. This is known as Pine Ridge, and it is an authentic stand of old growth. It was known as the finest example of virgin white pine in the eastern United States before the entire area was decimated by the blowdown of 1950. What remains is still impressive. The best way to see it is to ascend the ridge on an unmarked trail that takes off from an open grassy area on the shore known as Camp Johnny. Camp Johnny is one of the historic primitive campsites located along the river and available for public camping for up to three days without a permit.

The Robinson River descends to meet the Oswegatchie next, coming in on a series of rapids approximately a mile after Camp Johnny. Above here the going gets more difficult as the route of the river becomes encumbered with numerous beaver dams and blowdowns. Although the Robinson River is the last traditional spring hole, many small brook trout are still to be found upriver. Fishing for them can be a little difficult with the many alders arching over the river. The trout here are probably best fished for from the many beaver dams that now span the river. This same situation prevails along the lower reaches in areas where small spring creeks enter the Oswegatchie. In many instances the beaver have chosen the exact location where the bodies of water meet to erect the dam, and fishing the pool created by this dam is often good.

Several miles above the Robinson River, the Oswegatchie fans out into various separate feeder creeks and becomes basically unnavigable. Again, though, many of these feeders can be ascended for various lengths depending on water levels. At one time, the pond created by the huge beaver dam near the junction of these feeders was a mecca that beckoned trout fishermen from far and wide. There is still some good trout fishing present here today.

This concludes the Oswegatchie sojourn upriver. The trip downriver will definitely be quicker and may even reveal some Oswegatchie gems that remained hidden on the upstream paddle.

Headwater Ponds

There remains one final fishing opportunity in this fascinating area—the beckoning of the remote headwater ponds. Pursuing the wily trout in these forest-clad bodies of water offers perhaps the zenith in true wilderness fishing. Nestled deep in the forest preserve, they are reached only after long hikes on DEC-marked trails. The way is arduous as the ponds are best fished by boat, and the trek in will usually involve taking a lightweight canoe. No matter. Many consider it worthwhile, both for the tranquility earned and the splendor of the majestic forest traveled through. The difficulty here only enhances the wilderness experience.

Acid rain has affected these interior ponds more than it has Cranberry Lake or the Oswegatchie River. (See the discussion in the Introduction.) Those ponds with natural buffering ability have fared best. A number have also been temporarily improved by liming. Most suitable ones have been aerially stocked with brook trout by the DEC. Some large trout are still present in these ponds and are best caught by trolling or fly-fishing. Trolling is most productive in early spring, and many trollers favor lures with a worm trailing behind. During warmer weather, the areas of natural springs will have to be sought. The trout will be found congregating there. While increasing acidity has limited the percentage of juvenile fish surviving, 3- and even 4-pound trout are still present in some of these waters as ample reward for the energetic angler who undertakes the long hike back to them.

Following are a sample of some of the ponds that are still moderately productive. While there are others, these will serve quite well as an introduction:

- Cowhorn Pond. This 21-acre pond is reached by a hike of 6½ miles from a trailhead in the hamlet of Wanakena, or, alternatively, by a 4-mile trail from the southwest bay of Cranberry Lake, which can be reached via motorboat.
- Darning Needle Pond. This 30-acre pond can be reached only by a 2½-mile hike on a trail taking off from the southeast bay of Cranberry Lake. This trip can be done in combination with a day's fishing on Cranberry Lake.
- Tamarack Pond. Comprising 13 acres, this pond is reached by a hike of 8½ miles from the hamlet of Wanakena over the same trail used to reach Cowhorn Pond. In addition, the same alternative exists as at

Cowhorn, a 6-mile hike from the trailhead on the southwest bay of Cranberry Lake.
- Hedgehog Pond. This approximately 10-acre pond can be reached after a short ½-mile hike on a trail from the west shore of Cranberry Lake.

Other interior ponds productive for brook trout include Olmstead Pond, the beautiful Five Ponds, and fabled Cage Lake. Cage is reached only after a 9-mile trek from the village of Star Lake or an almost equally lengthy hike from the Oswegatchie River along the marked Five Ponds trail.

About the Author

A retired police officer, Peter O'Shea is a hiking guidebook author who lives in the town of Fine.

*Walleyes, like this one of trophy size, are an important part
of the menu of a Raquette River float-to-fish trip.*

CHAPTER SIXTEEN

The Raquette River: Highway through the Mountains

Tony C. Zappia

S tretching from Raquette Lake in central Hamilton County all the way north to its confluence with the St. Lawrence River east of Massena, the Raquette River offers a high-quality and varied outdoor experience. From large, crystal-clear mountain lakes to numerous white-water rapids and easy-flowing stretches of river, the Raquette is readily accessible by motor vehicle yet remote enough to set the stage for a true angling odyssey.

The Raquette undergoes several changes from lake to river along its course. Let's begin our discussion with Raquette Lake, its source.

Trout and Bass Fishing in Raquette Lake

Raquette Lake's physical features are impressive. It stretches over 5 miles in length and 3 miles in width and has a maximum depth of 96 feet. At 5,274 acres, Raquette is the eighth-largest lake in the Adirondacks. It has 99 miles of shoreline and numerous points, inlets, and islands.

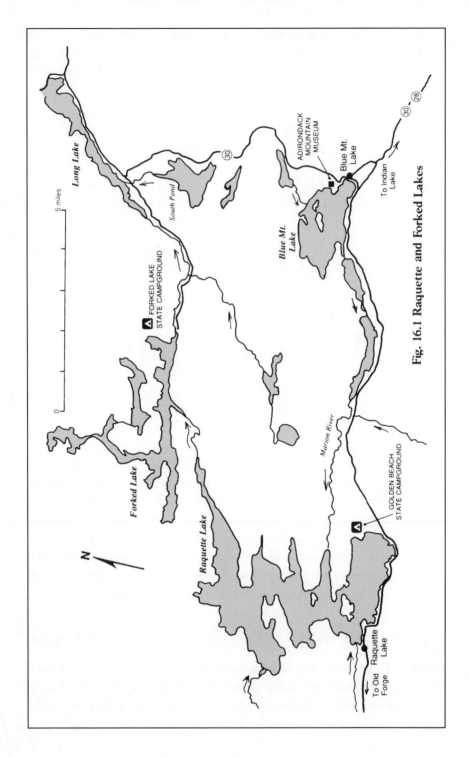

Fig. 16.1 Raquette and Forked Lakes

As soon as ice-out occurs, brook trout fishing from shore along NY 28 is often very good. Worms seem to be the brookies' favorite meal this time of year, and fish more than 2 pounds are annually weighed in at nearby bait and tackle stores. (In June 2009, the new modern-day state record brook trout was caught in Raquette Lake. Weighing 5.4 pounds, it was caught by Tom Yacovella using a Rapala plug.) When the weather warms, brookies will move deeper and may be found near spring holes and cold tributaries.

The second trout indigenous to Raquette Lake is important throughout the Adirondacks: the lake trout. Raquette Lake lakers serve as brood stock insofar as they supply eggs for the Chateaugay Fish Hatchery. At the same time, the Department of Environmental Conservation (DEC) annually stocks the lake with yearling lakers.

A boat is required to fish for lake trout. In the spring, trout can be taken in 30 to 50 feet of water by trolling flutter spoons with lead core line or copper wire. Downriggers are also used for deep trolling, and lighter line can be used. When concentrating on lakers, it is most important to fish the bottom and fish it slow. Midday (between 10 and 2) often produces the most fish.

As the water warms, lakers find their way to the deeper parts of the lake. At this time, trollers look to the north end, where maximum depth reaches 96 feet. The majority of fish will be found in 35 to 60 feet, and a depth finder would certainly come in handy to locate fish on the bottom near a structure or, occasionally, suspended.

Bass occupy a different niche here, and they are extremely plentiful. Although bass fishing can be good throughout the summer, Labor Day signals the beginning of cool weather and the best bass-fishing period. Smallmouths and largemouths begin to feed heavily and respond well to bait and lures. Both largemouths and smallmouths congregate along weed beds scattered along the lake, so look for deep water drop-offs that border these weed beds, and drop your offerings into 10 to 18 feet of water. Minnows and crawfish are the number-one and number-two baits. As for lures, Mr. Twisters, Rapalas, and top water lures such as the Zara Spook, Pop-Rs, buzzbaits, Jitterbug, Hula Popper, and smaller fly-rod poppers can all produce.

While bass and trout fishing may be more exciting, nothing will fill the freezer faster than a couple of days of perch and bullhead fishing. Bullhead can be taken from shore in early spring and fall by fishing mud bottom in 5 to 15 feet of water. Where you find lily pads along bays, you will usually find perch. Anglers need to offer worms to both perch and bullhead. Under the ice, perch will take a small minnow.

A small boat or canoe is not needed to take pails full of bullhead or perch, but for trout and bass fishing, a small- to medium-sized boat is required. A 12- to 16-foot aluminum or fiberglass shallow V-hull is ideal; the motor should be no smaller than 9.9 horsepower. Boat-launching facilities are scattered throughout the town of Raquette Lake. Along NY 28 there are four boat launches that will adequately handle a good-sized craft. Most marinas along the lake will serve the majority of your needs, from bait to boating supplies.

Forked Lake

Only ¼ mile from Raquette Lake and part of the same river system, Forked Lake is a medium-sized Adirondack lake spanning 1,248 acres with a maximum depth of 74 feet. Quite rocky, this lake offers both largemouth and smallmouth bass, as well as a good population of brook trout. Both perch and sunfish please the shoreline angler through those hot summer days.

As the days get warmer, brookies will move toward the northwestern part of Forked Lake. Here they will lie in deep holes during the day and move up to the surface at night to take a dry fly, either a real one or one with a hook in it.

Because Forked Lake contains so many rocky shoals and points, the smallmouth bass thrive, and many push the scales to the 4-pound mark. Smallies can be found early in the year along shallow rocky areas with weed beds. It seems as though the fish tend to favor the eastern end of the lake, especially near the outlet waters and near the state campground.

Largemouth bass do well in these waters. Plenty of weed cover offers old bucketmouth plenty of prime locations from which to launch an ambush. To successfully fish largemouths in Forked Lake, one should try rubber worms, spinnerbaits, Mr. Twisters, and various top-water lures. Best bets for locating largemouth are along the east end, where a rock ledge and weed bed are present. Shallow bays make up the west end of the lake, and largemouth are consistently taken here.

The only effective way to fish for bass in Forked Lake is out of a boat. Because the lake is relatively shallow, a boat rigged with an engine larger than 4 or 5 horsepower would be impractical. Most anglers prefer to use 16-foot canoes or small flat-bottom johnboats. At the Forked Lake Public Campground, anglers can launch a boat and park. There are 78 campsites surrounding the lake. The campsites can be had on a first-come, first-served basis.

Caution: Forked Lake runs west to east, and during strong west winds it can become quite dangerous for canoeists and others using small craft.

Buttermilk Falls

For those who choose to paddle their way from Forked Lake to Long Lake, the Raquette River drops 116 feet in 5 miles, and three carries must be made to reach the base of Buttermilk Falls. During the spring, brook trout can be taken by fishing at the mouths of feeder streams where they enter the Raquette. Brook trout can also be taken in the Raquette River between Raquette Lake and Buttermilk Falls. A 3-mile section above Buttermilk Falls is annually stocked with brookies during the spring. Worms and spinners work well, but the current will be fairly swift, and pools and eddies will yield the most fish. Canoeists are warned that the rapids above and below Buttermilk Falls are extremely dangerous during high water, and Buttermilk Falls is not runable.

The falls can be reached by motor vehicle from the village of Long Lake by traveling south on NY 28N/30 and turning right onto North Point Road. Buttermilk Falls parking area is located on the right side of the road and is approximately 5½ miles from the center of Long Lake.

The Raquette River

Anglers fishing out of canoes can resume their journey through the Raquette river system about ¼ mile from the base of Buttermilk Falls. The 4½-mile section of water upriver of the village of Long Lake is scattered with shallow bays of pickerelweed and pond lilies, which are home to great northern pike and both smallmouth and largemouth bass. Anglers who have smaller motorboats in the 14- to 18-foot class can launch at the state boat ramp, Town Dock Road, approximately ½ mile from Long Lake Town Beach. Also, there are many private marinas with boat launches along Long Lake where a minimal launch fee will be charged. For the angler without a boat, several places in Long Lake will rent small boats.

Long Lake

Long Lake is a fairly shallow, 14-mile-long lake with a maximum depth of 45 feet. Located in northeastern Hamilton County between NY 28N and

30, the lake is essentially a widening of the Raquette River. It flows roughly south to north, and prevailing summer winds favor downlake travel (south to north).

Northern pike are abundant in Long Lake. Their average weight is 3 to 4 pounds, although pike in the 10- to 15-pound class can be taken. One of the best areas on the lake for northerns is a place called Big Marsh. Located about 2½ miles north of the village, Big Marsh lies on the western shoreline directly across from Catlin Bay and is defined by a series of marker buoys. Anglers here cast Dardevles and sinking Rapalas, and use live bait early in the morning and later on in the evening. As the water warms, pike will migrate out into the deeper water, and anglers will find them in 15 to 30 feet. Other hot spots for northerns on Long Lake are the western bays just south of the Long Lake NY 30 bridge and the north marsh at the very foot of Long Lake.

Smallmouth and largemouth bass are concentrated along the north marsh. Because the lake is shallow, the warming of the water tends to play a critical role in fish behavior. Bigger fish will feed heavily at night and in early morning, and fishing Long Lake during midday is generally a waste of time. The only exception is during prespawn conditions. At these times in spring, both pike and bass can be caught any time of day by casting top-water lures close into shore, especially in shallow sandy or weed-filled areas.

When summer arrives, try the deep hole located at the north end of the lake. This 45-foot fish holding area will produce large northerns and bass trying to escape the tepid water temperatures associated with a shallow lake. If you have a boat equipped with a depth finder, look for suspended fish over deep areas and vertically jig for them. During the early morning and evening hours, concentrate your fishing along structure, such as islands, located adjacent to the 45-foot hole.

Pan fishermen can experience reasonably good perch and bullhead action just about anywhere in the lake. Most panfishing activity occurs around Big Marsh.

Marinas, hotels, stores, and restaurants are primarily located along the eastern shoreline. The south end of the lake is considerably developed, and the north end is mostly forest preserve.

The distance from the village of Long Lake to the north end is 9½ miles. While traveling downlake, you will see lean-tos scattered along the eastern shoreline that are available for use. During peak summer months, lean-tos will become less available because of the hundreds of canoeists traveling through the Raquette River system. If you plan on spending a few days and nights fishing the north end, it would be advisable to carry a tent.

Raquette Falls

As the river flows out of Long Lake, it forms a marsh, which empties into a slow winding network of islands and sandbars. A canoe or small motorboat can make its way through this 6-mile-long, slow-moving section of stream until the hills close in as you approach Raquette Falls. You must make a 1⅓-mile carry here in order to continue downstream.

Below (downstream of) the falls, pan-sized brown trout can be taken using worms, spinners, and various fly patterns. Each year, the DEC stocks a 1-mile stretch at Raquette Falls. This annual stocking currently takes place by air.

As the river descends some 80 feet, plunging over a rocky bed, the heavy rapids aerate the warm water at the base of the falls. This highly oxygenated water draws both cold- and cool-water species of fish. Your first cast with a crawfish can take a 2-pound brown, and your second cast can produce a 24-inch walleye.

The base of Raquette Falls is extremely productive for northern pike and smallmouth. Walleye averaging 18 to 24 inches during the spring also find their way to the base of the falls. Both pre- and postspawn walleyes can be tangled with here. Sinking Rapalas, deep-diving crankbaits, spinner/worm combos, or crawfish can draw good responses.

Below Raquette Falls

Still paddling downstream, we come to where the Raquette empties into Tupper Lake (Tupper Lake is discussed in chapter 6). As we leave Tupper Lake and head west on NY 3, we arrive at Piercefield about 7 miles later. Now fully harnessed for generation of hydroelectric power, the river from Piercefield Flow to Raymondville (65 miles downstream) is host to 20 dams and has been nicknamed the Workhorse River of the North. In spite of this great human intrusion on the lower Raquette, certain fishing opportunities have been created.

Piercefield Flow, the uppermost impoundment on this section of the Raquette, offers fishing opportunities in a pondlike situation. Anglers can take northern pike, smallmouth bass, an occasional walleye, and a variety of panfish. Below Piercefield and downstream to Carry Falls Reservoir is a very wild stretch of the Raquette, one that provides good fishing for small-mouth bass. Although presently used as a canoe route by white-water enthusiasts, the surrounding land is almost entirely private, and access is limited.

The Reservoirs

For the next 27 miles, beginning with Carry Falls Reservoir, the Raquette is no longer a river; rather, it is a series of eight reservoirs ranging in size from 122 acres to thousands of acres. Boat launch sites and campgrounds can all be found here. While it varies from reservoir to reservoir, angling is generally good. Walleye, northern pike, yellow perch, smallmouth bass, bullhead, and a variety of other panfish can all be taken in this stretch.

The largest of the reservoirs, Carry Falls—the fifth-largest lake in the Adirondacks—is located on NY 56 about 3 miles north of Sevey Corners. A blacktop road about a mile long connects this 6⅔-mile-long reservoir with NY 56.

The Parmenter campsite here offers anglers overnight sites for tents or trailers, as well as picnic tables, toilet facilities, drinking water, and fireplaces. The fee is minimal, and there is no charge for parking or day use.

After camp has been set, you may want to check on water conditions. Water levels can fluctuate as much as 20 feet in Carry Falls, and this will determine the day's fishing activities. As a rule, maximum water level occurs in late April through June, and minimum levels are encountered by late September.

Walleye are the favorite fish, and most anglers troll very slowly with a spinner/worm harness. This is tied to a three-way swivel with either 1 or 2 ounces of weight attached to the system, enabling the rig to bounce bottom. While trolling for walleye, it is common to hook into large yellow perch. These tasty fish can reach the 2-pound mark and are abundant here.

The head of Carry Falls Reservoir seems to be a favorite spot with anglers. Much activity occurs just below the rapids, where water is rich in oxygen and a bit cooler. Early morning and late evening should prove most productive.

Both spring and fall tend to produce the biggest stringers. There are large northern pike cruising the reservoir, so be prepared for bite-offs while fishing for walleye and perch. If you're after northerns, make sure you spool

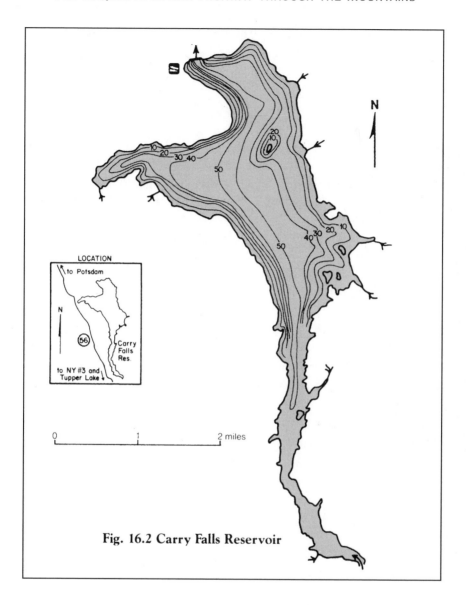

Fig. 16.2 Carry Falls Reservoir

up with at least 12-pound line, and if possible, tie on a heavier monofilament or wire leader for extra measure.

A word of advice from an old pro who fishes Carry Falls Reservoir: when trolling for walleye, make certain that you troll into the sun for best daytime results.

The final 63 miles of the Raquette winds its way through central St.

Lawrence County. It is still flowing essentially northward. The stretch of river from Raymondville to Massena produces good catches of smallmouth bass and walleye. Also, the occasional St. Lawrence River muskellunge can be boated during late spring and fall.

Like an old backcountry road winding its way through the mountains, bending to the left and then to the right, descending down a sloping, hilly, mountain pasture scattered with wildflowers, the Raquette River traverses more than 100 miles of the beautiful Adirondack region. For anglers and other outdoor lovers, it is truly a highway through the mountains.

About the Author

Tony C. Zappia was born and raised in Massena, New York. He is currently a freelance outdoor writer/photographer.

CHAPTER SEVENTEEN

Fishing Pole, Paddle, and Portage

Joe Hackett

The St. Regis Canoe Area

The St. Regis Canoe Area is one of the finest places in the Adirondacks to enjoy both paddle sports and angling adventures. The canoe area consists of 58 ponds and lakes, which were formed by glaciers. Even though the ponds lie very close together, they are often divided by steep eskers. Most of the ponds and lakes are located north of the old Remsen–Lake Placid railroad tracks, and the tract of land that contains the ponds is located roughly between the St. Regis Lakes and Upper Saranac Lake.

Within the St. Regis Canoe Area, motors of any kind are forbidden. There are several entrances to the area, all of which require portages. Most portages are no more than 100 yards in length, while some require a carry of over a mile. Portage trails are well marked with small white directional signs and are well maintained by the Department of Environmental Conservation (DEC). Fish Pond, which is accessible via a 5-mile journey on a well-maintained fire truck road, is also accessible via horse and bicycle.

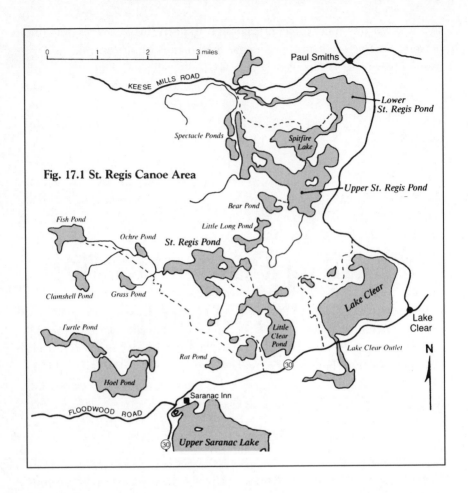

Fig. 17.1 St. Regis Canoe Area

Paddlers can easily travel from pond to pond while fishing each day from a central base camp. Camping in the canoe area allows anglers the opportunity to find which pond is producing on which particular day. Once into the area, a canoeing angler has dozens of options in planning a specific itinerary.

Travel and Fishing Tips

Travel in the St. Regis Canoe Area speaks well to the value of a lightweight canoe, and the Kevlar models are the finest. Tugging a heavy aluminum or ABS canoe over a 1-mile-long, buggy, muddy carry is not a good idea. Canoes or guide boats that are rigged with oars for rowing are a plus. Rowing allows for greater control, especially in windy conditions.

When trolling, it is essential to keep a slow speed to present the bait to the fish, but one must move fast enough to keep the bait from dragging bottom. Trolling spoons is a productive method for fishing for trout, and the most popular choice of anglers is a Lake Clear Wabbler, trolled slowly while trailing a snelled hook or leader behind. Anglers will attach either a night crawler or a streamer fly to the leader. Fly patterns such as a Mickey Finn, Hornberg, Grey Ghost, or Muddler Minnow are popular patterns for streamers. Trolling a streamer without the Wabbler requires that the angler twitch or sweep the rod to cause the streamer to dart like a wounded minnow. *Note:* The use of minnows or any fish as bait is prohibited on all of the St. Regis Canoe Area ponds. Most of the ponds have been reclaimed at least once to clean out all nonnative species of fish. It is the responsibility of all ethical anglers to protect our valuable natural resource.

Spinning rods should be medium action with 6- to 8-pound-test lines for trolling. Ultralight spinning rods with 4-pound-test lines are good for casting. Fly rods should be 7½ to 8½ feet in length and should take a 6- to 7- weight line, with a sinking-tip line, which is most useful for trolling.

Fly hatches are numerous and occur on a schedule that is similar to most Adirondack river hatches. The peak of the mayfly hatches is late May through early June, but sporadic hatches occur throughout the season. Using dry flies like a Black Gnat or Adams in size 14 or 16 at dusk is often productive. A favored technique is to drift the shorelines of these ponds and cast small ⅛- to ¼-ounce spinning lures along the shore. Watch for schools of fleeing minnows along the shorelines early and late in the day, and cast the lure in front of them. A slow retrieve with a twitch of the rod every few revolutions has produced many nice fish. Many lures will work, but good results are often had with Phoebes, Mepps, C.P. Swings, and Kastmasters, in gold or brass tone.

Bullhead, a fine eating fish, are plentiful in nearly all the ponds in the St. Regis Canoe Area and can be caught all night long with a hook, sinker, and worm that is cast out and left on the bottom.

Starting Out: Access

There are two public boat launch/parking areas at the eastern end of the St. Regis Canoe Area. One is located on Little Clear Pond, behind the Saranac Inn State Fish Hatchery off NY 30. (No fishing is allowed in Little Clear Pond, which is a brood pond for landlocked salmon. Nearby, Green Pond is also off-limits to fishing, as the pond is now used as a brood pond for raising lake whitefish, a species that once was common in many Adirondack lakes.)

*Canoeing in to fish the St. Regis area is one of the most popular
Adirondack trips. There are dozens of ponds to choose from.*

Access to St. Regis Pond, the largest pond in the area, is made via a 2-mile
paddle up Little Clear Pond, then a ¼-mile carry.

The other launch site is located off NY 30 on St. Regis Carry Road. The
parking lot is located on Upper St. Regis Lake, next to the private Lake
Shore Owners Association's boathouse and docks. It can often be over-
flowing with vehicles. Access from this launch requires a ½-mile paddle
across the Upper St. Regis Lake and several short carries through Bog Pond,
Bear Pond, and Little Long Pond.

The western end of the St. Regis Canoe Area is accessible via Floodwood Road, 4 miles west of the state hatchery on NY 30. Floodwood Road
divides the St. Regis Canoe Area from the Fish Creek–Rollins Pond
camping areas. It is also the dividing line between cold-water and warm-
water game fish species.

For access to this section of the St. Regis Canoe Area, a state launch is
located on Hoel Pond, adjacent to the Saranac Inn Golf Course. Putting in
on Hoel Pond requires a paddle of 2 miles across the pond and a carry over
the railroad tracks and into Turtle Pond. From Turtle Pond, one can paddle

into Slang Pond and carry over to Long Pond, or carry 1 mile into Clamshell Pond directly. From Clamshell, a ½-mile carry leads to Fish Pond.

Long Pond, which has a state launch on its western end, can be accessed via Floodwood Road just past the West Pine Pond turnoff. Long Pond has a decent population of smallmouth bass and is a starting point for trips to Ledge Pond, which holds lake trout, brook trout, and lots of perch. Also accessible from Long Pond are carries to Mountain Pond (brook trout) and the trail to Nellie and Bessie ponds, which requires a mile-long, very wet, carry. Long Pond produces some nice smallmouth bass and the occasional lake trout.

The East End
The St. Regis Canoe Area can be described in two sections: the east end and the west end.

The east end is centered around St. Regis Pond. It holds a good population of lake trout (18-inch minimum size limit), splake, and brook trout. It is best fished on calm days, as the wind can make for rough water because of the size of the pond. Trolling shorelines or casting spinners along the shore of the big island on St. Regis Pond is a good bet in the early season.

As the heat of the summer intensifies, fish deep, using copper or lead core line about 50 yards off the island. The east end of the canoe area also holds Little Long, Grass, Little Clear (no fishing), Bone, Bear, Bog, Ochre, Green, Meadow, Conley Line, and St. Germain ponds. The fishing on these ponds remains outstanding due to the effective fishery-management policies pursued by the DEC, and nearly all of these little jewels hold brook trout, and some hold lake trout, splake, and rainbows. Little Long Pond is well known for its population of splake and rainbow. The joy of observing large trout sipping big hexigenia mayflies at dusk is certain to make any fly fisherman smile.

Trolling, jigging, or casting spoons along the east shore of Green Pond, especially around the downed trees, will often produce fish. Another hot spot is along the small island on Little Long Pond, often a favorite location for shore fishermen who angle for rainbows throughout the evening.

Travelers should note that the eastern end of the St. Regis Canoe Area often endures heavy traffic. It is very popular with day-tripping canoeists, and during holiday weekends it can get very crowded. Overfishing in the early season can reduce fish populations, so catch-and-release fishing is stressed. Keep only enough for the evening meal, and you're sure to be rewarded in the future.

The West End

The west end of the St. Regis Canoe Area is centered on two large bodies of water, Long Pond and Fish Pond. Long Pond, which has been mentioned, offers access to Ledge, Mountain, Slang, Turtle, Ebony, Track, and Hoel ponds. While Hoel, Ledge, and Long ponds are stocked with brook and lake trout, the others hold decent populations of brook trout.

Between Long and St. Regis ponds lies Fish Pond, which has two lean-tos on its opposite shores. It produces some nice lake trout, along with a generous number of brook trout. The tranquility of this remote woodland pond is the reward most paddlers seek; the angling opportunities are simply a bonus.

Fish Pond is surrounded by Nellie, Bessie, Kit Fox, Mud, Sky, Little Long, Little Fish, Lydia, and Clamshell ponds. This section of the canoe area offers greater solitude than any of the other large ponds in the area. The arduous journey to Fish Pond tends to keep the day-trippers at bay. All of the ponds surrounding Fish Pond offer fine populations of brook trout, with Nellie, Bessie, and Clamshell ponds the clear favorites. Fishing pressure at this end of the area may be heavy at times, particularly in the spring and fall.

The shoals along the west end of Fish Pond offer particularly good opportunities for lake trout in the spring. This is certainly a place to practice catch-and-release. Take a couple of nice fish for dinner, and toss the rest back for future fishing fun.

Most of the Adirondacks' backwoods ponds are regularly stocked with heritage strain brook trout that can attain trophy sizes of 4 pounds or more.

JOE HACKETT

The Fish Creek Area

Adjacent to the St. Regis Canoe Area, but on the south side of the railroad tracks, is the Fish Creek–Rollins Pond State Campsite. The Fish Creek area offers a number of outstanding fishing opportunities for both warm-water and cold-water species. Operated by the DEC, the state campgrounds on Fish Creek and Rollins Pond are well kept and offer a fine base camp area for day trips to the numerous ponds surrounding this area. Also, Fish Creek–area ponds all feed into the Upper Saranac Lake, which has many primitive campsites located on its shores.

Boats with motors are allowed in many of these ponds, and access is often right off NY 30. (Boat and canoe rentals are located nearby at Hickok Boat Livery on Fish Creek Pond.) The fishing opportunities for smallmouth and largemouth bass are excellent, and there are enough northern pike available to keep things interesting.

Some of the better cold-water ponds are Follensby Clear, Horseshoe, Sunrise, Green, and Whey ponds. One pond that has consistently produced nice catches of bass and northern pike is Floodwood Pond, easily accessed via Floodwood Road off NY 30 at Saranac Inn. The pond can provide some furious smallmouth fishing with surface poppers or other lures along the shore around downed trees and stumps. It is one of the best, heat-of-the-summer bass ponds in this area. Trolling for northern pike can also be productive, especially at the western end of the pond near the channel to Rollins Pond.

Numerous roadside ponds are located in this area, and some hold decent populations of brook trout and rainbow. Whey Pond in the Fish Creek Campsite is a special-trout-regulations water (minimum length 12 inches, three fish per day, artificials only). It is known for its trophy rainbows and brook trout. Black Pond, located nearby, is also a good bet. Horseshoe, Sunrise, Echo, Rat, and Sunday ponds round out the list of brook-trout ponds.

Bass Fishing

Bass fishing has been an overlooked opportunity in the Adirondacks, mainly because trout and salmon are so readily available. The cold-water fisheries of the Fish Creek–Saranac area offer ideal bass habitat, as do the Upper and Lower St. Regis lakes and Meacham Lake. The shorelines of these waters offer rocky shoals and numerous downed trees, the type of structure that bass love.

There are very few fish I prefer to take on a fly rod more than a scrappy smallmouth bass. At the end of a hot summer's day, the smallmouth action can be outstanding. Using a small cork popper on a fly rod or a surface lure on a spinning rod, I prefer to seek fish that are prowling the shallow shorelines of the ponds. Casts made close to the shore, among the weeds and limbs, will usually get results. As the water calms toward dusk, the big fish are often taken in the shallow areas near drop-offs to deep water. Bass in the 2- to 3-pound range are available, and the occasional northern pike will often boil out of the water for a surface plug.

Best choices are cork poppers with rubber legs in green, black, or yellow, or surface Rapalas, Rebels, and frog imitations. Fishing crankbaits or lead-head jigs with rubber worms in the deeper water will produce fish in the heat of the day. Gary Yamamoto Senkos are a proven favorite. If bass aren't taking Senkos, it's time to quit.

Live bait such as crayfish or minnows, either trolled or cast with a bobber to shore, will do well, especially for pike. Unfortunately, pike will often take live bait very deep, which can make releasing a fish difficult. Although minnows produce well, many small pike are killed in the process of releasing them. Minnows should be reserved as a last resort.

The Bog River Flow Wilderness Area

This is an area that rivals the St. Regis Canoe Area for beauty and solitude. The Bog River Flow Wilderness Area, located in St. Lawrence County, just west of Tupper Lake, is accessed via NY 421 off NY 30 south of Tupper Lake. NY 421 goes around Horseshoe Lake and eventually melds to a dirt road that dead-ends at the state launch on Hitchins Pond.

This large wilderness tract includes the Bog River Flow, which connects Hitchins Pond, Lows Lake, Grassy Pond, Tomar Pond, and several other natural ponds. These ponds were flooded as a result of the creation of the upper dam on Lows Lake, a large and very shallow body of water. With an average depth of only 8 to 10 feet, Lows Lake is very susceptible to heavy winds and big waves. Even with a light wind the lake can form whitecaps, and with the prevalent western winds unblocked by any large mountains, Lows Lake can often be unnavigable by canoe.

The state boat launch at the lower dam leads upriver 2 miles to Hitchins Pond, another shallow body of water. Hitchins rarely gets as rough as Lows Lake, but it can offer a challenge. The Hitchins Pond flow contains brook trout, bass, and yellow perch; however, the trout are only fishable in the very early season.

As soon as the water warms enough for the perch to become active, an angler cannot get through the perch to get at the brookies. Yellow perch, some as large as 1½ pounds and 16 inches long, can provide plenty of action for the kids, and if prepared properly, they make a wonderful meal. They are easily caught on spinners or hook and worm.

A 100-yard carry at the head of Hitchins Pond leads over the upper dam and into Lows Lake. The first 7 miles up the flow are quite narrow and are

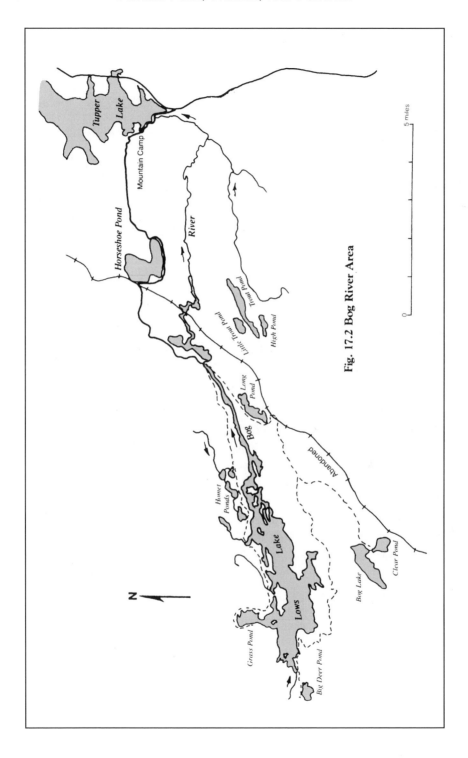

Fig. 17.2 Bog River Area

Lakes in the Big Woods

LITTLE TUPPER LAKE

Little Tupper Lake is part of the 1998 state land purchase. It lies within the William C. Whitney Area and is the home to the Little Tupper strain of brook trout. Little Tupper can be accessed from Circle Road, roughly 7 miles north of Long Lake village. There's a boat launch (no motors allowed) below the forest ranger base (formerly Whitney Headquarters).

Little Tupper is shallow for a brook-trout lake, with only two deep holes: one 37 feet, the other 18 feet. The best fishing is the first couple of weeks after ice-out and in September. Little Tupper is strictly catch-and-release fishing.

LAKE LILA

Eight miles beyond the forest ranger base, at the end of a 5H-mile drive down a dirt road, sits the Lake Lila parking area. There is a G-mile portage to the lakeshore put-in. Like Little Tupper, no motors are allowed on Lake Lila, but the lake is not strictly catch-and-release. The Lake Lila parking area holds only 30 cars, so if it is filled, you must park on Sabattis Road and carry your canoe the 5H miles; all land on each side of the dirt road is private.

Beautiful Lake Lila has good fishing for landlocked salmon (stocked), lake trout, and brook trout in the spring, and smallmouth bass during the warm months. Camping is allowed on four of the seven islands. There are also designated campsites on the mainland.

STILLWATER RESERVOIR

Stillwater Reservoir is a sizable backwater created by the damming of the Beaver River, which flows out of Lake Lila. Stillwater has some excellent smallmouth bass fishing and is also stocked with splake. There are some lake trout and brook trout as well.

The big reservoir is a fairly remote destination, and just getting to it can be an adventure. From Eagle Bay in the Fulton Chain, turn north off NY 28 onto Big Moose Road. After a little more than 6 miles, turn left at what is called Glenmore Corner, and continue on 1½ miles to Big Moose. The hardtop ends here. It is 10 more miles to Stillwater Road, where you turn into the forest ranger headquarters and the boat launch.

—Dennis Aprill

often windy. Once paddlers get beyond the Boy Scout camp on the east shore, the lake begins to widen until a second narrow passage is reached about 1 mile farther along. Passing through this channel, a view of Lows Lake proper is achieved, and paddlers are greeted with the usual whitecapped waves. Lows Lake is speckled with several beautiful islands, but camping is limited to a few numbered sites. The majority of the island campsites are reserved for Boy Scout use in June, July, and August.

Grassy Pond, located near the head of Lows Lake, offers true remoteness and a feeling of real wilderness. Grassy Pond Mountain, with its soaring cliffs, is a known nesting site for bald eagles. Eagles are often spotted on Lows Lake, along with a large number of loons, which breed in this area. Coyotes and owls usually are heard during the evening, and moose have been spotted in the area.

The fishing in Lows Lake, Grassy Pond, and the Bog River is not as good as it used to be for brook trout. Largemouth bass, accidentally introduced in the early 1980s, have nearly displaced brook trout throughout this waterway.

Because wind is so often a problem, trolling can be difficult, but it is effective. Spinners cast along shorelines can produce nice catches, as do poppers or jigs. Best bets are to cover shorelines in stumpy areas or along the cobblestone islands. The population of largemouth bass usually provides anglers with ample opportunities for a fish to fry.

Trout Fishing: Timing

I have found that trout fishing on the lakes and ponds of the Adirondacks falls into several distinct time frames in regard to peak production. Ideally, the best dates for fishing brook trout are right after the ice goes off the pond. Generally, this is late April or early May in the northern Adirondacks, but the depth of the snowpack and the extremes of winter temperatures can affect ice-out dates drastically. In a five-year span, ice-out on the ponds has ranged from March 28 to May 7. Predicting the date the ice will go is difficult at best; even so, the first weekend in May is often a safe bet for good fishing.

Brook trout feed heavily and respond favorably to nearly anything tossed their way during the first week to 10 days after ice-out. Unfortunately, this early feeding frenzy is followed by what I call the "two-week doldrums." Some ponds may produce for two days after ice-out, some as long as 10 days. But after this initial strong feeding period, the trout can then go off feed for

*Autumn trout fishing offers anglers the opportunity to catch
brook trout whose dazzling colors rival that of the fall foliage.*

as long as two weeks. The end of the doldrums is marked by the first few fly
hatches of the season, and the doldrums are over for sure once the dragon-
flies are in the air.

Consistently, the weekend of Mother's Day in early May has produced
the finest fishing of the year. Fly hatches continue throughout May and June,
and trout remain on the feed. As the heat of the summer comes upon the
ponds, the water warms, and trout seek deeper, cooler, more oxygenated
water. Often they congregate in the spring holes or near the inlets or outlets
of feeder streams on the ponds.

Usually, the depth of the water negates trolling, so still fishing is the order
of the day. July and August bring the warmest weather, and trout fishing is
reduced to early morning or early evening trips in search of rising trout. This
period need not be a fishless one, however, as bass and pike can be taken
readily in deep water during the day and along the shorelines at dusk.

The trout fishing picks up in September and is very good as cooler autumn evenings begin to lower the water temperatures through the close of the
season on October 15. Fat fall brook trout, dressed in brilliant spawn colors,
offer a splendid complement to the spectacular autumn foliage. The warm
days and cool nights of autumn make for enjoyable camping conditions.
There are few bugs and even fewer people in the woods after Labor Day.

About the Author

Joe Hackett has owned and operated Tahawus Guide Service since 1978. He grew up in Elizabethtown, New York, fishing the Boquet River. After earning a master's degree in recreation/outdoor education in 1980, Joe co-founded the New York State Outdoor Guides association, and today he specializes in fly-fishing remote ponds for brook trout. The St. Regis Canoe Area is one of the regions he knows best. He lives in Ray Brook with his wife and daughters.

Giant muskies like this still swim in the St. Lawrence,
where Arthur Lawton once took freshwater angling's most revered record:
a monster muskellunge 1 ounce short of 70 pounds.

CHAPTER EIGHTEEN

The St. Lawrence River: The Bountiful Boundary Water

Allen Benas

S erving as the common border between the United States and Canada for just more than 100 miles, the St. Lawrence River has beckoned to freshwater anglers in both nations for centuries. The majestic river, at 568 miles, is one of the longest in the continental United States and provides year-round fishing enjoyment for the whole family. The St. Lawrence River is named after the saint honored on the day of its discovery in 1615. It stretches from its source, the eastern end of Lake Ontario, northeasterly to the Gulf of St. Lawrence.

The river's recreational area is contained within the first 90 miles, from Lake Ontario to Massena, New York. From the village of Massena down-stream, the river is little more than a ditch as it leads to Montreal, Quebec City, and on to the Gulf. At its source at Lake Ontario, the river is more than

20 miles across. Dotted here by more than 1,700 islands of every size and description, it gradually narrows to only a few miles wide in its first 40 miles of flow. This expanse of water misled the earliest French explorer, Jacques Cartier, to name the region Lac Des Mille Isles, or Lake of the Thousand Islands. It is this section, now an extremely popular vacation and resort region, that has established the river as an angler's paradise.

The St. Lawrence Seaway has been referred to as one of the most dramatic engineering undertakings of the 20th century. With its completion in 1959, this conduit to the sea helped create the longest inland waterway on Earth. Ships from around the world now penetrate half a continent, while power generated by the great river supplies vast areas of both New York State and the Canadian provinces of Ontario and Quebec. From the standpoint of international commerce, the seaway opened the Great Lakes to direct ocean-going shipping traffic, linking all ports along the lakes—as far west as Duluth, Minnesota—to world markets. But environmentally, the seaway has been described by many as the worst thing that ever happened to the Great Lakes and St. Lawrence River—as it soon became clear that the benefits of world commerce did not come without cost.

At first, it was pollution. Ships discarded everything—ballast water taken on in the world's ports, garbage, and even bilge sludge and oil—into the river. Sewage too was a problem, as holding tanks were unheard of back then. As with our own U.S. and Canadian industry, the ships looked on our river and lakes as receptacles for any and all kinds of refuse and processed wastes. Environmental laws and strict enforcement have long since put a stop to these infractions, and the water now runs clean, clear, and surprisingly pure.

In the 1990s, the introduction of little mollusks called zebra mussels changed the water conditions. These were introduced in ballast water discharged from freighters entering the system from the Black Sea and proliferated at astonishing rates. Water once clouded by plankton is now crystal clear as each mussel filters as much as 2 liters of water a day. Where visibility was once limited to only a few feet, bottom is now visible as deep as 40 feet in early spring and late fall. Fortunately, nature has corrected for the imbalance by generating increased plankton hatches during the warmest months, allowing small fish to survive until their diet becomes smaller fish.

Weed growth has also changed. What were once huge weed beds dotting the river in depths of as much as 20 feet are now gravel bars littered by empty clamshells. Elsewhere in the river is a new kind of vegetation that accumulates in great masses of slippery, slimy weeds that look and feel like silk. As described by one botanist, the river is going through a transformation.

More recently the river, and all of the Great Lakes, has been invaded by the round goby. They too arrived in the ballast water of foreign freighters. They multiply at geometric rates, reproducing more than once a year. They are voracious eaters of smaller fish and eggs during the spawning period. They do have one upside, however; they are excellent food for larger fish such as perch, bass, northern pike, walleye, and muskie, resulting in a dramatic increase in the average sizes of these popular sport fish. Most recently, the viral hemorrhagic septicemia, or VHS virus, also considered an invasive species, has taken a toll of some species of fish, in particular, members of the pike family. The virus hit the hardest in the early 2000s, with attributable deaths declining by 2007.

To those simply intent on having an enjoyable vacation, the river offers unmatched scenic beauty, unlimited cruising opportunities, the certainty of catching fish, and a relaxed lifestyle that is unmatched by more confined and crowded vacation areas. To professional angling organizations such as the Bass Anglers Sportsmen's Society, the river is one of its most productive tournament locations. To muskie hunters the world over, the river is considered a mecca. A world-record muskie was taken here by Arthur Lawton in 1957 that reigned uncontested for 35 years.

Although populated by a wide array of freshwater fish, the river's reputation as a premier sport fishery focuses on four major species: great northern pike, smallmouth bass, walleye, and muskellunge. Seasons for these vary, so anglers can be on the river from early May through mid-March. As the river begins to run fresh in the spring, usually in early April, anglers anxiously await the opening of the northern pike season on the first Saturday in May. The success on opening day will depend heavily on what kind of spring the area had. A cold spring can set back the spawn, meaning that the mature pike could still be in the shallows of the marshes, safe from the angler's lure. A warming or "normal" spring beginning in early April means business as usual.

Although it is an immense water area, the St. Lawrence attracts boats of every size. Given calm winds and a sense of stable weather, anglers in boats as small as 14 feet are a common sight. Should the wind increase, the numerous islands offer shelter, and the waters surrounding them can be productive.

Pike

Knowledgeable pike anglers will seek out locations where they know there is underwater weed growth. With recent changes in the marine ecology, this knowledge is based on fishing experience during recent summers, where weed beds still grow close to the surface. The alternative is to fish much deeper in search of trophy pike that seek shelter from bright light in the river's depths and bottom growth.

The northern pike prefers to lie in hiding, awaiting the unsuspecting passerby. Like other members of the *Esox* genus, the pike is an ambush hunter. The most successful pike anglers will use large silver shiners, available locally (although imported from Arkansas). They are usually drifted just off the river bottom. Seldom will a pike pass up an opportunity for this tender morsel. Often, deep-running artificial lures are productive. Dardevle spoons, deep-running crankbaits, and jigs with worm and twister tails (either pork or plastic) have established reputable stature in the angler's northern pike arsenal.

Use ultralight to medium-weight tackle for pike. A good bet for a sporting encounter would be a light-action rod and reel with a capacity for at least 175 yards of 6-pound monofilament line. A stronger leader is suggested, not so much for pulling strength as for protection from pikes' ultra-sharp teeth.

Well-traveled anglers often compare northern pike fishing in the St. Lawrence with other areas. The consensus is that larger fish, although in smaller numbers, can still be caught farther north, in Canada. But when it comes to quantity, the St. Lawrence shines. Limit catches with an average size of 4 or 5 pounds (with occasional trophies in the 10- to 15-pound class) are routine.

Northern pike are a popular attraction for ice fishermen from freeze-up (usually in early January) until the season closes in March. Specimens as large as 20 pounds are not unheard of during the winter months, when the largest pike of the year are usually caught.

Popular wintertime northern pike hangouts can be found at Wilson Hill Causeway, between Louisville and Massena off NY 37B; Coles Creek Marina, between Waddington and Massena on NY 37; Brandy Brook, just east of Waddington on NY 37; the pulp docks in Ogdensburg (east of old Diamond National Plant); Perch Bay, outside Morristown off NY 37; and Chippawa Bay. In the Thousand Islands, ice fishing is done around Clayton and on Eel Bay and Lake of the Isles from Wellesley Island.

Early-season, open-water pike fishing can also be quite good in the waters mentioned, as they will produce numerous postspawn fish. Often overlooked, boat marinas offer outstanding early-season pike fishing. You can find marina facilities in nearly every community along the St. Lawrence. The season for northern pike extends from early May through March 15 of the following year. It then closes for seven weeks to allow for the spawn. The pike season is the longest of all sportfishing seasons on the river.

Smallmouth Bass

It is hard to say which fish is synonymous with the St. Lawrence: the muskie or the smallmouth bass. But there is no doubt that the smallmouth is far more abundant, being found in large numbers from Cape Vincent to Massena. No native needs a calendar to tell when the third Saturday in June has arrived. This is the heaviest-traffic day of the year, with cars, vans, campers, and boat trailers all heading for the river. Ask any old-timer along the river when the tourist season starts, and he'll more than likely say, "when the bass season opens!" Many things make bass the most sought after of all the river species. Above all, they are spectacular fighters. Pound for pound, they are the fightingest fish in fresh water, as the expression goes.

Throughout the summer months bass will move constantly, from day to day, even hour to hour. Weather fronts will affect them more than other species, as will sunlight and cloud cover. One day they will be deep, the next, shallow. You might catch them in 20 feet in the morning but have to go down 120 feet in the afternoon. Any self-professed "bass expert" you hear about along the St. Lawrence is probably giving himself a lot more credit than he deserves. Bass, simply put, are intimidating fish; they can make fools out of the best anglers. That's probably the main reason sports love to go after them.

The St. Lawrence Valley was created by glaciation during the last ice age, over ten thousand years ago. Consequently, there is no such thing as an average depth. With the deepest spot being nearly 300 feet, with adjacent islands only a few yards away, you can appreciate how a 30-foot boat can have its bow in 1 foot of water while anglers fish in 25 feet off the stern. Where modern crankbaits may serve well in impoundments, we have found it impossible to get them down to the 50-plus-foot depths that hold bass during the hot summer months.

Early in the season, while bass are still in the shallows, artificials can be very effective. After the fish move into deeper water, artificials are most practical in the evenings, when the bass move into the shallows to feed. Successful casting of artificials is done in depths ranging from a few to no more than 15 feet of water. Evening casting is best in bays or along the shoreline and around docks. The most popular artificials among visiting pros are jig-and-pig, medium-sized spinnerbaits, and small crankbaits.

As with pike fishing, the most successful anglers will use shiners. These 2- to 3-three-inch-long baitfish will produce more fish than all lures combined. Think of it this way: how can you improve on the fish's natural food?

As with pike, the best tackle for bass ranges from ultralight to medium weight. A good bet for a sporting encounter would be a light-action rod and reel with a capacity for at least 175 yards of 6-pound monofilament line.

Favorite smallie waters along the St. Lawrence can be found starting near Cape Vincent midway up the north side of Grenadier Island (especially after a north wind); the shoal on the northwest corner between Haddock and Grenadier Island (good late-summer fishing); Wilson Bay (south of Tibbetts Point Lighthouse); and the waters between Fox Island and the mainland. Moving east (downstream), numerous shoals, both shallow and deep, in the Clayton and Alexandria Bay areas hold large populations of bass.

Farther downriver, smallmouth bass can be found along any current break or weed bed between Morristown, Ogdensburg, Waddington, Louisville, and Massena. Pike and bass remain the most popular of the St. Lawrence fishes throughout the summer months.

Muskie

As mid-September approaches, with its shorter days and cooler nights, there is another group of anglers who begin to appear on the scene. Decked out in heavy garb, braving the chilled river in boats ranging in size from 16 to 25 feet, these anglers are in search of the ultimate freshwater trophy. These are the muskie hunters.

To some, the muskie is the fish of ten thousand casts; to others, the fish of a thousand hours. To no one is it an easy game fish. What makes the St. Lawrence still a choice muskie fishing destination? One reason may be that it holds the largest of the two remaining natural, or unstocked, strains of muskellunge left in North America. Another may be the knowledge that a world-record muskie came from this water. It was "on Sunday morning September 22 [1957]," the late Arthur Lawton wrote in his chronicle of the great fish in the June 1958 issue of *Outdoor Life*, "trolling off a small grassy island a few miles below Clayton, I hung and boated the biggest muskellunge ever landed on hook and line, a fish that on Monday evening, 30 hours after it was caught, weighed in at 69 pounds 15 ounces, 4 ounces heavier than the previous world record."

But anglers don't come to the river as intent on breaking Lawton's record as they are on setting their own. Perhaps they are after their first legal-sized fish, a personal record in itself. Maybe a 30-plus-pounder is what they're after—small perhaps in comparison to Lawton's, but a very respectable trophy nevertheless. Where 30-pound fish were trophies through the 1990s, 40-plus-pound fish are common today, with muskies over 50 pounds caught every year. Whether 20 pounds or 55 pounds, all of these are "records" of some sort when you are a muskie hunter.

The range of the St. Lawrence muskie, both as a species and individually, is the largest of all river game fish. They are found everywhere from Lake Ontario to Massena. The three most popular areas, however, remain the Thousand Islands region (where Lawton's record fish fell), around the city of Ogdensburg, and below the power dam in Massena.

In 1984 a study to learn more about the unique St. Lawrence River strain of muskellunge was initiated by the SUNY College of Environmental Science and Forestry at Syracuse. Netting in suspected spawning locations yielded several specimens. While most were scale-sampled, tagged, and released, nearly two dozen were fitted with small external transmitters. These radiotelemetry devices allowed biologists to trace the movements of the muskies in this vast waterway. What the biologists found was previously unsuspected by all but a few experienced muskie fishing guides. St. Lawrence River muskies are travelers; they are migratory. Mature fish tend to spawn in the same bays every year, but after the spawn they leave the area for larger ranges. Most Thousand Islands muskies summer in Lake Ontario. Fish that winter in Ogdensburg summer in the Thousand Islands, a much larger area of the river 60 miles upstream.

Part of the muskellunge strategy is timing. The most successful muskie fishing is done in the fall. The fish are at the height of their aggressiveness, gorging themselves in anticipation of lean winter months that lie ahead. Muskie mania prevails along the St. Lawrence from mid-September until the season closes in mid-December. By far, the vast majority of muskies are taken by trolling. Large lures are trolled at speeds that make them perform at the peak of their intended design. Many veteran muskie anglers will tell you, "it doesn't make much difference if the lure moves like a fish, as long as it moves like it's crazy." Every seasoned muskie fisherman I know contends that the color of a lure is secondary. It is the action that drives them nuts, and nutty fish make mistakes. The most successful lures have two or three sections and are 6 to 9 inches long. For years the majority of muskies were taken on the then-popular Creek Chub lures, which worked well with the heavy monel line that was used to get the lures down to depths of 20 feet. With the gaining popularity of downrigger fishing, allowing for much lighter tackle and thus more sport, these have now been replaced in popularity and performance by a multisectioned lure manufactured by the Radtke Bait Company. Although this lure takes most Thousand Islands muskies, lures such as the Believer, Depth Raider, and Rapala work well on downriggers, chalking up successes year in and year out.

Among the most popular muskie fishing spots along the St. Lawrence are the waters off Cape Vincent, including Featherbed and Hinkley Shoals. Downriver toward Clayton, anglers congregate on the famous Forty-Acre Shoals, Gananoque Narrows, and just west of the international bridge in the fast-flowing water adjacent to the shipping channel. Still farther downstream, the area around Chippewa Bay, although treacherous to even experienced boaters, is a known muskie hangout. Below Chippewa Bay you enter the Brockville Narrows, where muskie fishermen also converge. At Ogdensburg, most muskie fishing activity focuses on the sandbar where the Oswegatchie River empties into the St. Lawrence, just upstream from the international bridge. This is the only place along the entire river where most fishing is done at night. This rare occurrence stems from not only the movements of the fish (which come in to feed when the sun goes down), but also from the fact that the more prominent guides have day jobs and can only fish at night. Regardless, night fishing here produces.

The farthest east that muskie fishing is done is in Lake St. Lawrence, both above and below the St. Lawrence/Franklin Delano Roosevelt Power Dam located just outside Massena. Above the dam, muskie fishermen concentrate their activities near Coles Creek, Wilson Hill, and Long Sault islands. Below the dam, most muskie hunters key in on the tail race on the American side. Here numerous muskies are caught and released on a regular basis. Trolling one or two lures per angler, depending on whether you are fishing in Ontario or New York waters, fishermen follow underwater contours in depths ranging from 18 to as deep as 60 feet.

In recent years muskie fishing has improved dramatically. Many attribute the increased catches, particularly in the 50-plus-pound class, to the catch-and-release efforts started back in the early 1980s. Others contend that it is a combination of that and nature's evolutionary cycle, resulting in both good and bad hatch years. Regardless, days can be spent with not even a hit. On the other hand, occasionally a boat will limit out in only a few hours. Most dedicated muskie hunters do agree on one thing: in comparison to muskie fishing, a crapshoot is a sure thing!

Walleye

In addition to the species already mentioned, the upper St. Lawrence also holds a strong population of walleye. Because of a lack of angler pressure, walleyes have been allowed to multiply and grow to record-class size. Seven- and 8-pounders are average here, and 12- to 15-pounders are trophies (when is the last time you threw back a 6-pound walleye?).

The most successful spring walleye fishing is done in shallow bays in May and June by those casting Rapalas, small crankbaits, and jigs tipped with worms. During late July and August most activity is between the shipping channel and adjacent shallower areas, where the fish are intercepted with jigs and night crawlers as they head in to the shallows to feed in the dark. The most popular walleye spots are Carleton Island, near Cape Vincent and Fishers Landing, just west of the Thousand Islands Bridge.

Farther downriver, the mouth of the Oswegatchie River in Ogdensburg produces good catches of walleye. The waters between Waddington and Massena have also produced outstanding catches of large walleye. Of course, one of the premier walleye fishing grounds is below the St. Lawrence/FDR Power Dam. Here fishing is done exclusively from boats. Most walleye are concentrated in the tail race of the dam, and early morning and early evening seem to be the best times.

For nonangling members of the family, dozens of attractions will provide hours and even days of activity while the anglers enjoy their sport. The St. Lawrence River makes the area an international playground shared by Americans, Canadians, and visitors from around the world. They come to cruise, and they come to camp. Many come for the numerous attractions. But by far, most come to fish the waters of the bountiful boundary.

About the Author

Allen Benas is a member of the Outdoor Writers Association of America, the New York State Outdoor Writers Association, and the Pennsylvania Outdoor Writers Association. He has served as president of the Clayton–Thousand Islands Chamber of Commerce, charter member and first chairman of the Jefferson County Sport Fishery Advisory Board, member of the Fishery Committee of the International Joint Commission on the Great Lakes, and president of the Clayton Guides Association.

Benas has lived in the Thousand Islands section of the St. Lawrence River since 1950. He and his wife have operated the Thousand Islands Inn in Clayton, New York, since 1973. They also operate 1000 Islands Fishing Charters, the largest sportfishing charter service on the St. Lawrence River. Having spent the better part of his life on the river, Benas has been featured in numerous magazine and newspaper articles, as well as on television programs with regional, national, and international audiences. He is a recognized pioneer of downrigger fishing for muskellunge.

Resources

New York State Department of Environmental Conservation Offices in the Adirondacks

Region 5 Headquarters
Ray Brook, NY 12977
518-897-1200
Fishing hotline: 518-891-5413

Subheadquarters
Hudson Street Extension
Warrensburg, NY 12885
518-623-1200
Fishing hotline: 518-623-3682

Region 6 Headquarters
State Office Building
317 Washington St.
Watertown, NY 13601
315-785-2263

Subheadquarters
207 Genesee St.
Utica, NY 13501
315-793-2554